The Newlywed Table

A Cookbook to Start Your Life Together

Maria Zizka

PHOTOGRAPHS BY AYA BRACKETT

Artisan | New York

Copyright © 2019 by Maria Zizka
Photographs copyright © 2019 by Aya Brackett
Illustrations copyright © 2019 Mark Dingo Francisco

Library of Congress Cataloging-in-Publication Data

Names: Zizka, Maria, author. | Brackett, Aya, photographer.
Title: The newlywed table / Maria Zizka ; photographs by Aya Brackett.
Description: New York : Artisan, a division of Workman Publishing Co., Inc., 2019.
Identifiers: LCCN 2018030068 | ISBN 9781579657987 (hardcover : alk. paper)
Subjects: LCSH: Cooking for two. | Entertaining. | Newlyweds—Life skills guides.
    | LCGFT: Cookbooks.
Classification: LCC TX652 .Z59 2019 | DDC 641.5/612—dc23 LC record available
    at https://lccn.loc.gov/2018030068

Design and lettering by Graham Bradley

Artisan books are available at special discounts when purchased in bulk for premiums and sales promotions as well as for fund-raising or educational use. Special editions or book excerpts also can be created to specification. For details, contact the Special Sales Director at the address below, or send an e-mail to specialmarkets@workman.com.

For speaking engagements, contact speakersbureau@workman.com.

Published by Artisan
A division of Workman Publishing Co., Inc.
225 Varick Street
New York, NY 10014-4381
artisanbooks.com

Artisan is a registered trademark of Workman Publishing Co., Inc.

Published simultaneously in Canada by Thomas Allen & Son, Limited

Printed in China

First printing, March 2019

10 9 8 7 6 5 4 3 2 1

For Graham,
with all my love

CONTENTS

Introduction

A few months before my wedding, a friend sent me a letter. She had been married for some time and wanted to share a little secret. *The best is yet to come*, she wrote. I was overjoyed to be engaged to a wonderful guy, and we were having such fun planning our wedding. I felt as if life couldn't possibly get any better, so how could the best be yet to come?

But slowly I started to realize she was right. Graham and I married, moved into a new apartment, and set out to make our home a cozy and welcoming space. We were cooking a lot—for ourselves, for each other, and for family and friends—and in the process of learning how to be together in our new kitchen, we were figuring out even more about each other and our relationship. During our first months as newlyweds, there were moments when I felt closer to my husband than ever before—and they often occurred in our kitchen.

We had enjoyed eating and cooking together since we met in college, but over the years, we learned some valuable lessons and skills. On one of our very first dates, I invited Graham over for dinner at my apartment, a tiny one-bedroom at the edge of campus. I'll never forget the menu: winter squash soup, warm whole Dungeness crab, and sautéed Brussels sprouts. Yes, Brussels sprouts! I must've been too nervous to consider that Brussels sprouts don't exactly scream "romance." Despite my questionable choice of side dish, I had the best time sitting at the table late into the night, eating slowly, laughing, and getting to know Graham. We would go on to cook frequently for each other and to cohost many dinner parties and brunches for our friends. By graduation, we were writing a weekly recipe column for the student newspaper, and in the years that followed, we spent as much time in the kitchen together as we could.

· · ·

There are countless ways to express love through food, and my hope for this book is that it gives you the tools to feel confident cooking for and with the person you adore. Whether you're newly engaged and beginning to dream about making a home together or you've been living under the same roof for a while, it is never too early or too late to cook together.

Cooking is, at its core, a way to nourish yourself, but it is also a creative, satisfying endeavor and a learning process. Cooking with someone you love is all that, times two. It can also be doubly messy. You'll most certainly encounter roadblocks, moments when everything isn't going according to plan. That's all very normal and nothing to worry about. If something goes wrong, don't lose heart— check out "Common Cooking Issues and How to Fix Them" (page 285). As you read this book, you'll learn how to plan ahead as much as possible, how to put together a balanced menu, and how to host with grace and warmth.

An important goal to keep in mind is that cooking at home should be a pleasure. Of course, sometimes you just need to eat, but other times you can linger and really enjoy the process—it's key to learn to cook so you can do both. When you cook together, share all the responsibilities. Learning to cook with someone you love requires unselfishly covering for their slipups and gracefully recognizing when they cover for yours. Celebrate everything, even (and especially) the success of a delicious weekday dinner for just the two of you. Always hold on to your sense of humor. Things happen. Do not beat yourselves up if a dish doesn't taste exactly as you'd hoped, and never apologize for food you've cooked. Not every meal will be perfect, but perfection is not the point—your home is not meant to be a restaurant; it is a place to feel at ease, to gather with the people you love, and to have fun together.

Cooking as a couple can be incredibly romantic, but it's also worthwhile for its practicality. Buying groceries and cooking meals at home will always be more affordable than going out to eat. Whenever possible, consider making a double batch of a recipe so that you can have leftovers stashed away in the refrigerator, ready to be enjoyed. Packing a lunch is a terrific way to save money and also a sweet thing to do for someone.

As you begin your life as a newly married couple, you'll figure out your own way to divide household tasks. For too long, the duties of cooking fell to the wife. This is a ridiculous default, because a person's gender has nothing to do with that person's aptitude for cooking, and a marriage in which both partners work full-time is not at all unusual—plus, spending time in the kitchen and creating meals with another person is more enjoyable. Let's do away with any notions of who should be responsible for cooking and start with a clean slate. You're in this together. You're a team.

Keeping teamwork in mind, you'll quickly find that there are certain aspects of cooking and entertaining that one of you enjoys more than the other. For example, some people loathe washing dishes, but plenty of others don't mind it. You may love making cocktails for friends, while your partner may prefer baking dessert or shopping for groceries. You're probably both capable of chopping an onion, but one of you might enjoy it more or be able to accomplish it faster than the other person can. It's up to you as a couple to figure out who ought to take out the trash, put away the clean dishes, rinse the lettuce, make the coffee or tea, and so on, all based on what makes the two of you run smoothly as a team. Be honest with each other, and remember that things change over time and no two couples are the same.

This book gives you all the recipes you need to start your life together: weeknight dinners, meals to entertain the in-laws, menus for holidays and other celebratory occasions like your anniversary, and much more. The chapters are organized by level of difficulty and serving size, from recipes for two to meals for up to six or eight. "Dinners for Two" (page 22) includes fast and easy recipes for weeknights and slightly more involved yet still straightforward recipes for weekends. Next are chapters with recipes for vegetarian main dishes (page 56) and side dishes (page 82) to serve with your meals. Once you've gotten the hang of cooking for each other, you'll feel more confident cooking for friends and family. "When Company Comes Over" (page 112) shows you how to create elegant and fun dinners for special nights, while "Sweets" (page 146) covers celebratory and everyday desserts alike. "Breakfast Anytime" (page 178) has recipes you can serve in the morning or at any hour of the day. You might turn to "Snacks" (page 208) when it's just the two of you at home and you're craving a small bite. On weekends and holidays, when you have plenty of time, try one of the longer recipes—bread, jam, even kimchi—in "Kitchen Projects" (page 232). The final chapter of the book, "Little Extras" (page 264), contains all kinds of specialty foods, items that aren't strictly necessary but are fun embellishments to your cooking. Throughout the book, interspersed between the chapters, are bonus recipes and tips on everything from cooking outdoors (page 176) to caring for kitchen tools (page 260), as well as sample menus and game plans for parties (page 142).

• • •

With every meal comes dirty dishes, but I'd like to make a case for the peace of cleaning up together. After a romantic dinner for two or a festive gathering of friends, there's something so satisfying about sharing a glass of wine as you take turns scrubbing and putting away pots and pans. It's in these quiet, special moments, as Graham and I talk about the night, reminisce, or plan for our next party, that I feel most thankful for the man I love and for every chance I have to cook with him.

Your first years together as newlyweds will be sweeter than you can possibly imagine. There's much to celebrate: birthdays, anniversaries, holidays, and more. Through it all, you'll have the love of your life by your side, and together you can do anything. I wish you every success and joy on the delicious adventure you're about to have! Don't sweat the small stuff, and always remember that the best is yet to come.

Kitchen Equipment and Tools

Set up your kitchen with a solid foundation of essential equipment—the basic pots, pans, and small tools you'll use regularly. It's much better to invest in just a few high-quality, durable tools that'll last for years, maybe even a lifetime, than it is to outfit your kitchen with every new gadget on the market. And while there will often be two of you in the kitchen, you won't need two of everything.

In addition to prioritizing durability, look for kitchen tools made from natural materials like wood, stone, cotton, and glass. You'll be preparing food on these surfaces, and these materials can be cleaned easily and won't leach any unwanted chemicals into your food. Factor in the beauty of each piece of equipment. If it's going to sit out on your countertop, it should be pleasing to the eye. If possible, hold every tool before purchasing it to determine whether it feels good in your hands. You'll be more inclined to cook if your kitchen looks inviting and your tools are a joy to use.

Once you and your partner start cooking together, you'll find a rhythm and begin to discover which dishes you enjoy cooking often. At that point you'll have a clearer sense of which nonessential tools you might like to add to your collection. Take it slowly and try to leave room in your cupboards for a special addition. It's fun to pick up a fluted ravioli cutter on your travels to Italy, or an earthenware tagine in Morocco, or a beautiful timeworn madeleine pan at a flea market in Paris. Tools like these also make thoughtful gifts for wedding anniversaries and birthdays.

As for precisely what is and isn't essential, it might be helpful to consider the staple meals you'll cook at least once a week, and then work backward from there. For many, that means pasta, salads, soups, and braises, the occasional roasted chicken, and lots of sautéed vegetables. Here's a list of useful kitchen tools.

ESSENTIAL EQUIPMENT

Bottle Opener and Waiter's Friend–Style Corkscrew

Don't bother with fancy and expensive corkscrews. There's a good reason every waiter at every restaurant uses the same simple style of corkscrew to open a bottle of wine.

Box Grater

For hard cheeses and other ingredients, such as carrots, zucchini, and potatoes.

Cast-Iron Skillet
(10 or 12 inches/25 or 30 cm in diameter)

These are best inherited or purchased used, because years of cooking builds up a nonstick surface inside the skillet. Look for used cast-iron skillets at garage sales, and don't worry if they look a little worn-out and rusty; they can almost always be revived. If you decide to go the route of buying a new skillet, it should be quite affordable and will last you decades, if not longer. (For more about how to season, clean, and care for cast iron, see page 260.)

Chef's Knife (8 inches/20 cm long)

For chopping, slicing, and dicing.

Colander

Mostly for draining pasta, but also useful when you need to rinse vegetables and fruits.

Fine-Mesh Sieve

For straining sauces and stocks.

Half Sheet Pans
(18 by 13 inches/46 by 33 cm)

Made of thick yet lightweight aluminum, these rimmed baking sheets will become your kitchen workhorses. Use one to bake a dozen cookies, to roast vegetables, or as a tray upon which you can set all the necessary tools for frying. Even after years of hard use, these pans never warp or rust. Pick up a couple at a restaurant supply store or cookware store.

Kitchen Towels

You'll want a stack of these. They can be used in place of pot holders to grasp hot handles. Although white towels are beautiful, I find they quickly become stained with turmeric, beets, or red wine. No matter the color you choose, kitchen towels will need to be replaced semiregularly, any time they still look dingy or feel oily after a run through the washer and dryer.

Ladle

To serve soups and to scoop up broths and sauces.

Large, Heavy-Bottomed Stainless-Steel Stockpot (6 to 8 quarts/6 to 8 L)

Good for making soups and stocks.

Loaf Pan
(8½ by 4½ inches/11 by 21 cm/1.5 L)

Ceramic, metal, and glass all have their benefits. Ceramic loaf pans are usually the best looking, so you can take them right from oven to table. Metal loaf pans, which are typically aluminum-coated steel, will last you a long time. Glass loaf pans offer the same perk as glass pie dishes, in that you'll be able to see breads and cakes, like Poppy Seed Loaf (page 157), browning as they bake.

Long Serrated Bread Knife

Unfortunately, you cannot sharpen serrated edges, which means this knife will dull with time. Since you'll likely want to buy another one at some point in the future, choose a reasonably priced serrated knife and put more of your budget toward the straight-bladed chef's knife and small paring knife.

Measuring Spoons and Cups

Choose both a liquid measuring cup (1-cup or 2-cup/240 or 480 ml capacity) and a set of nesting dry measuring cups. Technically the liquid and dry cups hold the same volume, but each is designed to more accurately measure wet and dry ingredients, respectively. You'll also need a set of measuring spoons—from 1 tablespoon down to ¼ teaspoon.

Mixing Bowls

Choose a set of nesting bowls in various sizes.

Mortar and Pestle

There's no better tool for pounding garlic cloves to a smooth paste. A mortar and pestle can also be used to easily crush whole toasted spices to a powder, and you'll never have to worry about replacing the batteries like you do with a spice grinder. Bigger mortars are easier to work in, but the price can increase in relation to size. A heavy marble 1-cup (240 ml) capacity mortar should get the job done.

Muffin Tin (12 well)

For both muffins and cupcakes. A curved edge on at least two sides helps you easily grasp the tin when you're taking it out of the oven or rotating it on the oven rack.

Paring Knife
(2 to 4 inches/5 to 10 cm long)

For cutting smaller ingredients like strawberries and for making precise cuts.

Pepper Grinder

Freshly ground black pepper is what you want. Avoid the preground kind; it's not nearly as flavorful.

Pie Plate/Dish

Choose any material you like. A glass pie plate gives you the advantage of being able to see how dark the sides of a crust are getting while the pie is in the oven.

Quarter Sheet Pans
(9 by 13 inches/23 by 33 cm)

As endlessly useful as half sheet pans but in a smaller size that comes in handy when roasting nuts or seeds in the oven, or when baking just two Chocolate Chip Cookies (page 150) for a late-night treat.

Rasp-Style Grater

For citrus zest, nutmeg, and fresh ginger.

Rolling Pin

The long French-style wooden rolling pins without handles (sometimes tapered at the ends) look handsome, feel nice under your hands, and are easy to clean. (A persuasive argument could be made that this tool is not essential. If you don't have one, a wine bottle will work in a pinch.)

Round Cake Pans
(9 inches/23 cm in diameter)

Buy two identical pans so you can make layer cakes.

Rubber Spatula

To scrape down the sides and across the bottom of a bowl of cookie dough.

Small Stainless-Steel Saucepan
(1 to 2 quarts/1 to 2 L)

For steaming rice and for boiling two servings of pasta.

Tongs

A humble but useful tool for flipping steaks in a skillet.

Vegetable Peeler

Simple is best here. Y-shaped peelers have a devoted following, but the regular swivel blades work just fine, too.

Whisk

Look for a whisk with stiff spokes. As for its size, a medium whisk will whip successfully in a medium bowl. Tiny whisks are cute but not all that practical.

Wire Rack

Look for one made of stainless steel that fits perfectly inside a half sheet pan.

Wooden Cutting Boards

As large as will fit on your countertop and as heavy and immovable as you can afford. It's useful to have at least two boards: one reserved exclusively for fruit and rolling out dough, and the other for prepping everything else, including chopping garlic and onions, which will leave traces of their presence. (For more about cleaning wooden cutting boards, see page 261.)

Wooden Spoons

Great for stirring, because they won't scratch your pans.

NONESSENTIAL (BUT USEFUL) EQUIPMENT

Blender

You might consider starting with an immersion blender before buying a countertop blender. Handheld versions are usually more affordable, and they work well, if not quite as speedily.

Dutch Oven

Choose a large one that can hold at least 5½ quarts/5 L.

Food Processor

The spinning blade of a food processor makes quick work of chopping nuts, blending pesto, and, with a special attachment that comes standard on most models, even slicing vegetables.

Food Scale

Check out the recipe for Chocolate Chip Cookies (page 150) for an introduction to using a food scale in the kitchen. It's way easier than you might imagine, and it's the surest way to bake with precision.

French Steel Pan

Sometimes called an omelet pan or a crêpe pan, a French steel pan comes preseasoned with a coating of beeswax, which acts as a nonstick surface ideal for cooking eggs.

Ice Cream Scoop

For scooping frozen desserts without bending the handles of your spoons.

Instant-Read Thermometer

Good for taking the internal temperature of roasts so you know exactly when they're done.

Medium Saucepan (3 quarts/3 L)

If you already have a large and a small, this saucepan will complete the set.

Pastry Brush

The ones with rubber bristles are simple to clean and won't shed when you're brushing beaten egg on the edges of a Leek and Goat Cheese Tart (page 63) or across the top crust of a Caramel Apple Pie (page 171).

Rice Cooker

You don't absolutely need a rice cooker because you can steam rice in a regular pot on the stovetop. (For the recipe, see page 60.) However, rice cookers do a fabulous job of perfectly cooking rice every single time.

Salad Spinner

For the best-tasting salads, make sure to thoroughly dry the salad greens and herbs before dressing them. A spinner will do this for you quickly and efficiently.

Spider Strainer/Skimmer

Look for a stainless-steel one with a long bamboo handle—it should cost only a few dollars. You'll use it to lift fried foods out of hot oil, skim the surface of chicken stock, and scoop cooked ravioli out of boiling water.

Stainless-Steel Sauté Pan (12 inches/30 cm in diameter)

Cast-iron skillets are fabulous for cooking nearly everything, but they can impart a metallic taste to acidic foods. When you're making tomato sauce or adding a splash of lemon juice or vinegar to a dish, it's better to use a stainless-steel sauté pan rather than cast iron.

Stand Mixer or Handheld Mixer

You can beat butter and sugar together by hand with a wooden spoon, but it's so much easier and faster with a mixer. Use the whisk attachment to quickly beat egg whites for Lemon Meringue Kisses (page 153) and also to whip cream in a matter of seconds.

Stocking the Pantry

Once you've collected the essential kitchen equipment and tools, the next order of business is gathering some ingredients. Stock your pantry with everyday staples like salt, spices, and oil, ingredients you'll rely on for a wide variety of dishes. It's worth buying the best-quality pantry essentials you can afford because they will enhance every dish. A well-stocked pantry is a good cook's secret weapon. Using just the following items, you can prepare quick, satisfying meals anytime.

Anchovies and Capers

Try to buy both anchovies and capers salt-packed, a method of preserving that best retains their flavor and texture. If oil-packed anchovies and brine-packed capers are all that's available, don't worry; just check the ingredients list to make sure there aren't any additional preservatives, which can lend strange flavors. No matter how the anchovies and capers are packed, rinse them thoroughly before adding them to a dish. For whole anchovies on the bone, soak them in cool water for a few minutes to soften them, then gently lift the two fillets off the center bone, remove the fins and tail, and rinse away any scales. Anchovies are a key ingredient in Caesar salad, and they're fabulous on pizza. Capers can be chopped if they are large, but it isn't necessary to do so.

Even a tiny spoonful of capers gives a big boost of flavor to pasta, herb sauces, and frittatas.

Baking Powder and Baking Soda

Look for an expiration date on the container, as these leavening agents do lose their gusto over time. Even better, buy small quantities of baking powder and baking soda from the bulk foods aisle at the grocery store, and replace them often.

Black Peppercorns and Other Whole Spices

Dried spices can add intrigue and nuance to a dish, but only if they are freshly ground. Instead of stocking your pantry with store-bought preground spices, seek out whole spices sold in bulk, and buy them in the smallest quantity you can get away with. We have a set of tiny glass jars, each labeled with the name of the spice it contains. Any time a recipe calls for a ground spice, I toast the whole spice in a dry pan over medium heat until it smells fragrant and looks a shade darker, then I grind it to a powder using a mortar and pestle. Yes, it takes extra time, but the flavor is well worth it.

Canned Tomatoes

Look for organic whole peeled tomatoes. You can use them as they are, chop them by hand, or puree them into a sauce using a blender.

Dried Beans

Beans are affordable and highly nutritious. Stock a couple of standard types like black beans and cannellini beans, and make sure to try cooking other varieties you may not have tasted.

Dried Chiles

These add heat and smokiness to all kinds of dishes. You can use relatively mild peppers like ancho and New Mexico chiles or super-fiery peppers like chiles de árbol. For information on the different types of chiles, plus a recipe for homemade hot sauce, see page 267.

Dried Pasta

Any shape you like—short, long, curly, straight. The suggested boiling times on the back of the box are almost always too long. Start tasting to see if the noodles are done cooking several minutes before instructed. You can always boil them a little longer, but once they're overdone, there's no going back.

Flour

Both all-purpose and whole wheat flour are useful to keep on hand. Stock smaller quantities of other whole-grain flours, like buckwheat, so that you can make blini (see page 122) and crêpes (see page 188).

Oats and Other Whole Grains

There's a wide and fascinating world of grains to explore, including farro, barley, quinoa, sorghum, buckwheat, bulgur, freekeh, spelt, amaranth, and teff.

Olive Oil

You'll want to have two different types of olive oil. Both should be extra-virgin, cold-pressed, and high-quality. One is your everyday olive oil for sautéing vegetables, while the other should be reserved for finishing dishes. In other words, the first is a cooking oil and the second is meant to be enjoyed raw. There are many wonderful olive oils. Taste before buying, if possible, and you'll soon learn whether you prefer oils with peppery flavors, green vegetal aromas, or perhaps delicate, fruity notes. Your everyday oil should be more affordable and less nuanced in flavor than your finishing oil. Store olive oil in a cool place, out of direct sunlight.

Polenta and Cornmeal

Polenta is coarsely ground corn, whereas cornmeal is typically much finer. It's worth seeking out freshly ground polenta and cornmeal, which have bright flavors and are becoming easier to find.

Rice

Rice comes in three sizes: short-grain, medium-grain, and long-grain. Short-grain varieties are used for making sushi, medium-grain varieties (like arborio, Vialone Nano, and Carnaroli) are best for risotto, and long-grain varieties (like basmati and jasmine) have a firm, nonsticky texture that is perfect for pilaf.

Salt

Keep two different types of salt in your kitchen. The one you'll reach for most often is fine sea salt. Choose sea salt free of iodine and any anti-caking agents, which impart unappealing flavors. You want the salt to have a texture that makes it easy to sprinkle evenly over vegetables and meats and to stir into soups. Not too coarse and not too fine, either; sort of the consistency of cornmeal. Sometimes sea salts will look a little gray or a little pink, have inconsistent coloring, or feel slightly damp. All are signs of natural production, which is a good thing. The second type of salt you'll want is flaky sea salt. It will be your finishing salt, a coarse, crunchy pop to sprinkle over a dish just before serving.

Sugar

For baking, keep on hand granulated sugar, brown sugar, and confectioners' sugar (also called powdered sugar). You might also consider a coarse-textured finishing sugar such as turbinado sugar for sprinkling over piecrusts.

Vanilla Extract

Purchase only pure vanilla extract, made without artificial vanillin. If you can find whole vanilla beans, it's easy to make your own vanilla extract and vanilla sugar (see page 280 for the recipes).

Vinegar

Signs of good, unpasteurized vinegar include cloudiness, a cluster of beneficial bacteria (called the "mother") floating on top or growing near the bottom, and a dark bottle. Heat and light will harm vinegar, so store it next to the olive oil in a cool place, out of direct sunlight.

Dinners for Two

To learn how to cook as a couple, get in the kitchen and get started. Don't let any worries slow you down. Start small with dinner for just the two of you. On weeknights, when you'll likely be rushed and hungry after a long day, how about comforting bowls of tomato soup and grilled cheese sandwiches? Or diner-style burgers that you can cook in less than ten minutes? On weekends, you might consider taking your time and roasting a chicken or making risotto with the season's best produce. The more often you cook together, the better cooks you'll become, and the more confident you'll feel cooking for and with each other.

Roasted Tomato Soup and Grilled Cheese

Serves 2

This is a humble and comforting dinner for a weeknight, and a terrific recipe to begin with if you're just starting to cook. The tomato soup is a bit more involved than the grilled cheese, so it's best to work together on the soup first, then one of you can make the grilled cheese while the other sets the table and finishes the soup.

Tomato Soup

1 (28-ounce/795 g) can whole peeled tomatoes, with juices

3 tablespoons olive oil

Fine sea salt and freshly ground black pepper

2 slices bacon

1 small yellow onion, diced

2 teaspoons fresh thyme leaves

2 garlic cloves, thinly sliced

3 cups (720 ml) water

¼ cup (60 ml) heavy cream

Grilled Cheese

Unsalted butter

4 slices country-style bread

¾ to 1 cup (85 to 115 g) grated cheddar cheese

Make the tomato soup: Preheat the oven to 500°F (260°C).

Cut the tomatoes in half and arrange them cut-side up in a baking dish in which they fit snugly in a single layer. (It's no big deal if the tomatoes are soft and falling apart.) Drizzle the olive oil and any juices in the can over the tomatoes. Season with ½ teaspoon salt and several grinds of pepper. Roast for 30 minutes. (Don't worry if the tomato juices burn a little around the edges—those darkly roasted bits will add deep flavor to the soup.)

Meanwhile, in a large, heavy-bottomed pot, cook the bacon over medium-low heat until browned and crisp. Using tongs, transfer the bacon to a paper towel–lined plate and let cool. (Reserve the bacon as a garnish for the soup, or eat it as a little snack while you finish cooking.) Add the onion, thyme, and ¼ teaspoon salt to the pot. Cook over medium heat, stirring occasionally, until the onion is golden brown around the edges, 2 to 3 minutes. Add the garlic and cook for no more than 1 minute, just until fragrant but not browned. Scrape the roasted tomatoes into the pot. Add the water and ¼ teaspoon salt. Bring to a simmer and cook for about 10 minutes. ⟶

Meanwhile, make the grilled cheese: Spread a generous amount of butter on both sides of the bread slices. Heat a large skillet over medium heat. (If all 4 slices don't fit in the pan, you may need to use two pans or cook one grilled cheese at a time.) Add the bread to the pan and cook until golden brown on the first side, 2 to 3 minutes. Use a spatula to flip the slices over. Arrange the cheese on 2 of the slices, making sure it evenly covers the entire surface of the bread. Place the other 2 slices on top of the cheese. Set a small weight such as a ramekin on top of each sandwich. (Alternatively, gently press down on them with a spatula.) Cook until golden brown, about 1 minute, then flip, reapply the weight, and cook until the second side is golden brown and the cheese has melted, 1 to 2 minutes.

When the soup is done, puree it directly in the pot using an immersion blender or carefully transfer it to a countertop blender and puree. (If using a countertop blender, work in batches and remember to remove the center of the blender lid, then cover the hole with a kitchen towel to avoid steam buildup.) Stir in the cream and season the soup with salt and pepper.

Serve the tomato soup and grilled cheese together.

Variation

VEGETARIAN TOMATO SOUP

Leave out the bacon and cook the onion in 2 to 3 tablespoons butter.

Money-in-the-Bank Breaded Chicken

Serves 4

When this breaded chicken emerges from the oven, it's crisp and browned yet still juicy inside. I learned the recipe from my mother-in-law. She calls it "money-in-the-bank chicken" because having breaded chicken leftovers in the fridge gives her the comfort of knowing a delicious lunch or dinner is never too far away. Ask your in-laws what their money-in-the-bank dish is—everybody has one—and work it into your repertoire. Not only will your partner feel the comfort of a familiar meal, but you'll also gain a go-to dinner, and you can't ever have enough of those. *Pictured with Quick Slaw (page 96).*

2 large eggs

Splash of half-and-half or milk

2 garlic cloves

Fine sea salt and freshly ground black pepper

1½ cups (160 g) panko or finely ground bread crumbs

¼ cup (60 ml) olive oil

¼ cup (15 g) chopped fresh dill

¼ cup (15 g) chopped fresh flat-leaf parsley

¼ cup (15 g) chopped fresh chives

1 pound (450 g) boneless, skinless chicken breasts

1 pound (450 g) boneless, skinless chicken thighs

Preheat the oven to 400°F (200°C).

In a wide, shallow bowl, whisk the eggs and half-and-half. Using a mortar and pestle or the back of a large knife, pound the garlic and a pinch of salt to a smooth paste. Stir the garlic paste into the egg mixture along with another pinch of salt and a few grinds of pepper.

In another wide, shallow bowl, mix together the panko, olive oil, dill, parsley, and chives, stirring until the panko crumbs are evenly moistened with the oil. Season with ½ teaspoon salt and lots of pepper.

Pat the chicken dry with a paper towel and cut into 2-inch (5 cm) pieces. Dip each piece first in the egg mixture, then in the seasoned panko, rolling to coat all sides evenly. Place the coated chicken pieces in a single layer on a rimmed baking sheet. (They should all fit, but you may need to play Tetris to arrange them.)

Bake for 20 minutes, until golden brown on the undersides, then flip and bake until cooked through, 5 to 15 minutes more. Serve hot. ⟶

What to Do with Leftovers?

CHICKEN SANDWICHES

Cut the breaded chicken into bite-size pieces and make a sandwich on a soft roll with a good amount of mayonnaise or Aioli (page 273) and a tall stack of lettuce, plus a dash or two of Hot Sauce (page 267, or store-bought).

CHICKEN TACOS

Warm a couple of corn tortillas and pile bite-size pieces of breaded chicken in the middle, along with a handful of fresh cilantro leaves. Other welcome additions to the tacos include Lime Crema (page 271) and Quick Slaw (page 96).

CHICKEN PARM

Place the breaded chicken pieces in a baking dish in a single snug layer. Drape a thin slice of prosciutto over each one, followed by a slice of mozzarella. Spoon store-bought tomato sauce or Red Sauce (see page 30) over the top, then sprinkle with a generous amount of grated Parmigiano. Cover the dish with aluminum foil and bake in a preheated 325°F (160°C) oven until the chicken is hot in the center and the mozzarella has melted.

Simple Pasta and Red Sauce

Serves 2

Tomatoes are acidic and need to be balanced by a generous amount of fat. In cooked tomato sauce, olive oil works well, as does butter, but bacon fat has richness along with robust flavor. You can include a number of additional ingredients in this quick red sauce—pitted olives, fresh parsley, capers, anchovies—although none is necessary. Keep a can of tomatoes and a box of dried pasta in your pantry, plus some bacon in your freezer, and you'll have all you need for a simple and comforting dinner any time you need one.

Red Sauce

2 thick slices bacon

½ yellow onion, diced

2 garlic cloves, sliced

Fine sea salt

1 (14-ounce/400 g) can whole peeled tomatoes, with juices

Handful of fresh basil leaves

1 tablespoon olive oil

8 to 10 pitted Castelvetrano or Niçoise olives (optional)

1 small bunch flat-leaf parsley, chopped (optional)

2 tablespoons capers, rinsed (optional)

2 anchovies, rinsed (optional)

Pasta

½ pound (225 g) dried pasta of any shape

Freshly grated Parmigiano-Reggiano cheese

Make the red sauce: Use clean kitchen scissors to cut the bacon crosswise into pieces about ½ inch (1.5 cm) wide. In a large pot, cook the bacon over medium heat until browned and crisp, about 8 minutes. Using a slotted spoon, transfer the bacon pieces to a small bowl, leaving the bacon fat in the pot. Add the onion to the pot and cook, stirring with a wooden spoon, until softened but not browned, about 4 minutes. Add the garlic and cook for 1 minute. Stir in a few pinches of salt and the tomatoes with their juices. Fill the tomato can about halfway with water and pour it into the pot. Toss in the basil. Bring to a simmer and cook, stirring occasionally to break up the tomatoes, until thickened, about 15 minutes.

Meanwhile, make the pasta: Bring a large pot of salted water to a boil. Add the pasta and cook until al dente. (Ignore the instructions on the package because they are almost always wrong. Instead, taste a noodle after 5 minutes, and again every minute thereafter. The pasta is done when it tastes soft but still has a chewy resistance when you bite down. If you cut a noodle, you'll see a tiny speck of white in the center.)

To preheat serving bowls, ladle some water from the pot into the bowls.

When the pasta is done, reserve 1 cup of the pasta cooking water, then drain the pasta and transfer it directly to the pot of sauce. Set the pot over medium-high heat, add half of the reserved pasta water, and cook, stirring often, until the sauce coats the noodles, 1 to 2 minutes. There should be a little liquid pooling at the bottom of the pot. If there isn't, add more pasta water until there is. Stir in the olive oil and any (hopefully all!) of the optional sauce ingredients. If you didn't add olives and/or capers, you may need to season the pasta with a pinch or two of salt.

Pour out the water in the bowls and serve the pasta in the warmed bowls, with grated cheese on top.

Variation

GREEN SAUCE

Instead of a red sauce for the pasta, you can make a simple green sauce. This recipe was inspired by Joshua McFadden, the chef at Ava Gene's in Portland, Oregon, whose own version was inspired by Rose Gray and Ruth Rogers of the River Cafe in London. Start by bringing a large pot of salted water to a boil. (You'll use it to cook the greens and then boil the dried pasta.) In a small pan over medium-low heat, cook 2 garlic cloves that have been smashed with the back of a large knife in ¼ cup (60 ml) olive oil along with 1 teaspoon of fennel seeds, stirring often, until the garlic is fragrant and slightly golden, about 2 minutes. Transfer to a blender. Boil 4 cups (4 ounces/115 g) stemmed kale leaves or spinach leaves until just tender, about 5 minutes for kale and only 1 to 2 minutes for spinach. Use tongs to transfer the greens to the blender. Add 1 large bunch of stemmed basil and ⅓ cup (45 g) pine nuts. Blend on high speed until very smooth, adding a splash of cooking water from the pot as needed to get the blender going. Taste and season with salt and pepper. Cook the pasta as instructed in the recipe, reserving 1 cup (240 ml) of cooking water, drain, and return the pasta to the dry pot. Add a big spoonful of the green sauce along with a splash of the reserved water and stir to coat the noodles, adding more green sauce as desired. Serve with lots of grated Parmigiano-Reggiano cheese on top. (Any leftover green sauce is wonderful spread on sandwich bread with salami and sliced provolone cheese.)

Risotto for Any Season

Serves 4

Risotto has a reputation for being finicky, but I promise it's simple and takes less than thirty minutes. This recipe makes an autumnal mushroom risotto; see the other seasonal suggestions on the next page and feel free to improvise. Start by preparing the vegetable you plan to mix in, then make the risotto, and combine the two just before serving.

Mushrooms

4 cups (220 g) mushrooms, such as chanterelle, oyster, or shiitake

2 tablespoons olive oil

1 tablespoon unsalted butter

2 teaspoons fresh thyme leaves

½ teaspoon fine sea salt

Risotto

3 cups (720 ml) chicken broth (see page 47) or vegetable broth

3 cups (720 ml) water

Fine sea salt

3 tablespoons olive oil

1 small yellow onion, finely chopped

1½ cups (300 g) short-grain risotto rice, such as arborio, Vialone Nano, or Carnaroli

¼ cup (60 ml) dry white wine (or about 1 tablespoon vinegar and 3 tablespoons water)

1 tablespoon unsalted butter

Freshly grated Parmigiano-Reggiano cheese

Freshly ground black pepper

Fresh thyme leaves, for garnish (optional)

Make the mushrooms: Wipe the mushrooms with a paper towel to remove any dirt. Cut or tear them into bite-size pieces and discard any tough stems. Heat a large skillet over medium-high heat for 2 minutes. Add the oil and butter. Once the butter has melted, add the mushrooms, thyme, and salt. Cook, stirring only once or twice, until browned on both sides, 6 to 7 minutes.

Meanwhile, make the risotto: In a medium saucepan, bring the broth and water to a simmer. Taste for seasoning, adding salt ¼ teaspoon at a time until the mixture tastes as salty as soup. Be careful not to overdo it; you can always add more salt later.

Heat a large pot over medium heat. Add the olive oil, onion, and ½ teaspoon salt. Cook, stirring frequently, until the onion is softened, about 4 minutes. Stir in the rice and cook for a few minutes, until lightly toasted and fragrant. Pour in the wine and cook until it evaporates. Using a ladle, add about ½ cup (120 ml) of the warm broth to the pot. Cook, stirring occasionally, until the rice has absorbed the liquid ⟶

and thickened, about 5 minutes. Continue adding the broth ½ cup (120 ml) at a time, letting the rice absorb all the liquid after each addition and stirring often to prevent the risotto from sticking. The risotto is done when the rice is tender but retains a slight firmness at its core, like al dente pasta. (You may not need to add all the broth; on the other hand, if you run out of broth and the risotto isn't done yet, add hot water ½ cup/120 ml at a time until it is.)

Remove the risotto from the heat and stir in the mushrooms. Add a final ½ cup (120 ml) of the broth, the butter, and a handful or two of Parmigiano. Let the risotto rest for 2 to 3 minutes, then stir vigorously until the risotto becomes creamy. The texture should be a little loose but not watery. Taste for seasoning, adding salt and pepper as needed.

A shower of chopped fresh thyme on top is nice but not necessary. Serve immediately—risotto waits for no one.

Seasonal Variations

SPRING RISOTTO

Substitute 2 cups (300 g) green peas for the mushrooms. The peas are already tender, so you only need to sauté them in a pan with ¼ cup (60 ml) water and 2 tablespoons unsalted butter for a few minutes.

SUMMER RISOTTO

Substitute 2 large heirloom tomatoes for the mushrooms. Chop the tomatoes into bite-size pieces and place in a medium bowl. Season with a couple of big pinches of fine sea salt, a few grinds of black pepper, and 1 to 2 tablespoons olive oil.

What to Do with Leftovers?

RISOTTO CAKES

Use your hands to shape the cooled risotto into balls about the size of a small lime. Dredge gently in cornmeal. In a skillet, heat 2 tablespoons olive oil over medium heat and panfry the risotto cakes until golden brown and warmed through. Serve with fried eggs.

Diner-Style Burgers and Oven Fries

Serves 2

You can make a terrific burger in less than ten minutes. Cooking it at home means you're able to customize the burger exactly how you like it. If you know your partner loves pickles, slice a few extra for him or her. If, like me, you love ketchup, mustard, *and* mayonnaise on a burger bun, then go right ahead and add them. We can all agree that fries and burgers are true soul mates. Making fries will take you a bit of time, so you should start with the fries, maybe accompanied by a rousing discussion of which toppings you believe belong on a proper burger.

Fries

1 pound (450 g) Russet potatoes, scrubbed

1 tablespoon olive oil

1 teaspoon paprika

½ teaspoon fine sea salt

Freshly ground black pepper

Flaky sea salt

Burgers

½ pound (225 g) ground beef (75 to 80% lean)

1 tablespoon neutral-flavored oil, such as grapeseed or canola

Fine sea salt and freshly ground black pepper

2 cheese slices (optional)

2 hamburger buns, sliced in half

Toppings of your choice: ketchup, mustard, mayonnaise, sliced pickles, red onion, avocado

Make the fries: Preheat the oven to 450°F (230°C). Place a rimmed baking sheet in the oven while it preheats. (The hot pan will discourage the potatoes from sticking.)

Cut the potatoes into ½-inch-thick (1.5 cm) wedges. Toss them in a large bowl with the olive oil, paprika, fine salt, and lots of pepper. Wearing oven mitts, remove the hot baking sheet from the oven and carefully spread the potatoes over it in a single layer. Roast until browned and maybe even a little charred in a few places, about 15 minutes. Flip and roast until tender inside, 5 to 10 minutes more.

Meanwhile, make the burgers: Divide the meat into 2 equal balls and set them on a plate. You want the meat to be cold when it goes into the skillet, so refrigerate it for about 5 minutes, if needed. ⟶

Heat a large cast-iron skillet over high heat for 1 minute. Swirl in the oil and heat until it shimmers. Place the balls of meat in the skillet and use a spatula to press down on each, squashing it into a 4-inch (10 cm) patty about ½ inch (1.5 cm) thick. Cook for 2 minutes. Sprinkle with salt and pepper.

Flip the patties and top each with a slice of cheese (if using). Cook on the second side until cooked to your desired doneness, about 1 minute for medium. Transfer the burgers to a clean plate. Add the buns to the pan, cut-side down, and immediately turn off the heat. Toast the buns, letting them turn golden brown and crisp from the residual heat, about 1 minute.

Assemble the burgers with your favorite toppings. When the fries come out of the oven, sprinkle with flaky salt. Serve the burgers with the hot fries on the side.

Variation

SWEET POTATO FRIES

You can use any kind of potato for the fries. To make sweet potato fries, cut the potatoes into wedges and season with the spices and oil. Roast in the oven for 10 minutes, then flip over and continue roasting until tender inside, about 10 minutes more. Sweet potatoes will cook faster than other kinds of potatoes.

Schnitzel, in a Hurry

Serves 2

For the tastiest schnitzel, seek out high-quality, pasture-raised meat. It costs more, but it's absolutely worth it. If you don't like pork, you can use beef, chicken, or even a thin fillet of fish. Don't shy away from using the proper amount of butter and oil in the pan—the schnitzel needs to swim in the hot fat in order to become crisp all over.

½ cup (60 g) all-purpose flour

Fine sea salt

1 large egg

¼ cup (60 ml) heavy cream

½ cup (55 g) bread crumbs

⅓ pound (150 g) boneless pork loin or pork shoulder, fat trimmed

Freshly ground black pepper

3 tablespoons unsalted butter

3 tablespoons olive oil

Lemon wedges, for serving

Fresh flat-leaf parsley, for garnish

Set up a schnitzel dipping station: On a large plate, toss together the flour and ¼ teaspoon salt. In a pie dish, whisk together the egg and cream. Spread the bread crumbs across another plate.

Cut the pork into two pieces. Place one piece between two sheets of parchment paper and pound the meat as thin as you possibly can without creating any holes. (A meat mallet is the ideal tool, but a wine bottle, rolling pin, or small, heavy pot will work.) Repeat with the second piece. Season the pork with salt and pepper on both sides.

In a large, heavy skillet, melt the butter with the oil over medium-high heat. Working with one cutlet at a time, dredge the meat in the flour mixture, shaking off any excess, dip it in the egg-cream mixture, then coat it gently with bread crumbs. Place the meat in the skillet, tilting the pan and spooning fat over the top. Cook until the bread-crumb coating puffs and starts to brown, about 1 minute. Flip and cook on the second side, continuing to spoon fat over the meat, until nicely browned. Transfer the schnitzel to a paper towel–lined plate. Repeat with the second cutlet, using the fat that's already hot in the pan.

Garnish with lemon wedges and parsley and serve right away.

Got Spinach or Kale? Add a big handful of rinsed spinach greens or stemmed kale leaves to the hot pan after you've cooked the meat. The residual heat will cook the greens in about 2 minutes for spinach and 3 to 4 minutes for kale, and the leftover fat will flavor them.

Cast-Iron-Skillet Steak with Blue Cheese Butter

Serves 2

A cast-iron skillet is the right choice of pan for cooking a steak because you can safely preheat it until it's so hot it's nearly smoking, and it will retain that heat, leading to an evenly browned steak with lots of flavorful juices sealed inside. Cooking steak indoors does create a lot of smoke in your kitchen, so open the windows and, if you can, remove the battery from the smoke detector (but please don't forget to put it back after dinner!).

1 boneless beef steak (about ¾ pound/340 g), such as rib eye, flat iron, strip, or hanger

Fine sea salt and freshly ground black pepper

1 ounce (30 g) blue cheese, crumbled, at room temperature

3 tablespoons unsalted butter, at room temperature

1 teaspoon olive oil

Flaky sea salt

Use paper towels to pat the steak dry—this will ensure proper browning. Generously season both sides of the steak with fine salt and pepper, then let the steak rest at room temperature for at least 15 minutes.

Meanwhile, in a small bowl, use a fork to mash together the blue cheese, 1 tablespoon of the butter, and a few grinds of pepper.

Heat a large cast-iron skillet over medium-high heat for 3 to 4 minutes, until very hot. Swirl in the oil and the remaining 2 tablespoons butter. Place the steak in the skillet and cook until browned on the first side, about 3 minutes. Flip and cook on the second side to your preferred doneness, 3 to 4 minutes for medium-rare. (If using a thermometer to check doneness, 130°F/55°C is medium-rare.) Use tongs to hold the steak on its side and crisp any strips of fat for another minute or so. Transfer the steak to a plate. Spread the blue cheese butter on top of the steak, tent with aluminum foil, and let rest for about 10 minutes. (You don't have to use all the blue cheese butter if you don't want to; any that doesn't melt is delicious spread across toast.)

Sprinkle a pinch of flaky salt over the steak and serve.

Easiest Undressed "Salad" Rinse and dry two handfuls of arugula or watercress and serve alongside the steak.

Yours and Mine Pizza Night

Serves 2

Making pizza at home is easier than it sounds, especially if you don't worry about making the dough. Ask your local pizza place if they'll sell you enough dough to make one pie. No need to buy premade sauce, because the best sauce can be made in a matter of seconds simply by blending raw canned tomatoes with a splash of olive oil and a big pinch of salt. All that's left to figure out are the toppings. In the spirit of love and compromise, you can customize the pizza by adding your favorite toppings to one side and your partner's favorites to the other.

Olive oil

1 (1-pound/450 g) ball store-bought pizza dough, at room temperature

1 (14-ounce/400 g) can whole peeled tomatoes, with juices

Fine sea salt

Pinch of red pepper flakes

4 ounces (115 g) fresh mozzarella, sliced ¼ inch (6 mm) thick

3 to 5 fresh basil leaves

Other optional toppings: pepperoni, olives, anchovies, sliced onion, mushroom, bell pepper

Preheat the oven to 500°F (260°C).

Drizzle a little olive oil on a rimmed baking sheet and use your hands to spread it across the surface of the pan. Stretch and gently pull the pizza dough into a large circle and place it on the baking sheet. Once you let go, the dough will shrink back into a smaller circle—give it a chance to rest for a minute, then gently stretch and pull it again, repeating the resting-and-stretching process until the dough is as large as possible without tearing.

In a blender or food processor, combine the tomatoes and their juices, 2 tablespoons oil, ½ teaspoon salt, and the red pepper flakes and blend until smooth.

Spoon some tomato sauce over the pizza and use the back of the spoon to spread the sauce in an even layer, leaving a ½-inch (1.5 cm) border. (Store leftover sauce in an airtight container in the refrigerator for up to 3 days or in the freezer for up to 6 months. You can add it to Roasted Tomato Soup, page 25, or use it in red sauce for pasta—see page 30.) Scatter the mozzarella, basil, and any other toppings of your choice across the pizza. Bake until the crust is golden brown and the cheese is lightly browned in a few places, 12 to 15 minutes. Cut into slices and serve.

Roasted Chicken and Potatoes

Serves 4

If you're working on this as a couple, divide and conquer the preparation of the chicken, a process that involves a frustrating amount of hand-washing if done alone. Seasoning raw meat with salt and pepper is much easier with two sets of hands! Make sure to start well ahead of time by seasoning the chicken the night before you plan to roast it; whoever gets home first can take the chicken out of the fridge to warm up before it goes into the oven.

Fine sea salt

Freshly ground black pepper

2 teaspoons paprika

1 small (3½- to 4-pound/1.6 to 1.8 kg) whole chicken

2 large handfuls of fingerling potatoes (about 1½ pounds/680 g)

The night before you plan to roast the chicken, place a large piece of parchment paper on a cutting board for easy cleanup. Pile 1 heaping tablespoon salt on one side and grind lots of pepper next to the salt. Mix the paprika into the salt and pepper. Cut an approximately 8-inch-long (20 cm) piece of kitchen twine and set it on the parchment.

If there are any giblets or a neck inside the chicken, discard them. Pat the chicken completely dry with paper towels. Set the chicken on the parchment.

Sprinkle about half the salt mixture inside the chicken. Turn the wing tips under and secure them under the bird so they don't burn in the oven. (I always think of this motion as the same one we sometimes do when we are sunbathing—arms raised, fingers intertwined behind the head—and it always makes me laugh to imagine a chicken sunbathing.) Pull the chicken legs together and tie the twine tightly around the drumstick tips in a secure knot. Trim any excess twine. Sprinkle the remaining salt mixture evenly over the top and sides of the chicken, pressing the spices into the skin. Transfer the seasoned chicken to a plate, cover loosely, and refrigerate overnight.

The following day, remove the chicken from the refrigerator and let it come to room temperature, at least 1 hour and up to 3 hours. About 15 minutes before you're ready to roast the chicken, preheat the oven to 450°F (230°C). →

Place the chicken breast-side up in a cast-iron skillet, roasting pan, or Dutch oven. Nestle the potatoes around the chicken and season them with a few pinches each of salt and pepper. Roast for 50 minutes, stirring the potatoes around in the chicken fat after about 30 minutes. Check for doneness by cutting the skin between the breast and the thigh; the juices should run clear. If the meat between the breast and thigh still looks pinkish-red, return the chicken to the oven and roast for another 10 minutes or so. The potatoes should finish cooking at the same time as the chicken.

When the chicken is done, transfer it to a large plate or dish and let rest for at least 15 minutes and up to 30 minutes. This is a crucial step, not to be skipped, because it gives the juices a chance to become evenly distributed.

To carve the bird, first remove the twine. Grab a drumstick tip and twist and pull the leg away from the body while making short cuts with the tip of a knife through the skin that connects the leg to the body until the leg is cut free. Repeat with the second leg, then set the two legs on a platter. Cut down the center of the breasts, along both sides of the center bone. Pull the breast meat away from the center bone and use the tip of your knife to help you remove each breast as one piece. Cut crosswise into thick slices. Serve warm.

Three Meals in One   This recipe shows off the ways in which a single chicken can provide more than just one meal. You can serve the roasted chicken for dinner one night, eat leftovers on a sandwich for lunch the next day, then make broth with the bones.

What to Do with Leftovers?

CHICKEN SALAD

Cut leftover chicken meat into bite-size pieces and place in a bowl. Add about ½ cup (30 g) chopped tender fresh herbs, such as tarragon, basil, flat-leaf parsley, and/or chives, plus any other ingredients you like in chicken salad: 1 finely chopped celery stalk, 1 or 2 thinly sliced scallions, a handful of halved grapes, maybe some chopped walnuts. In a small bowl, stir together the juice of ½ lemon, 1 small spoonful of Dijon mustard, 1 large spoonful of crème fraîche (store-bought, or see page 271 and leave out the lime), and 2 large spoonfuls of Aioli (page 273) or mayonnaise. Season with fine sea salt and freshly ground black pepper.

Add the sauce to the chicken and stir until well mixed. If you have a good amount of chicken meat or you'd like the chicken salad to be more coated with the sauce, stir together more lemon juice, mustard, crème fraîche, and aioli, keeping the proportions about the same as before. When you're happy with how the chicken salad tastes, make open-faced sandwiches on slices of dark rye or sourdough bread.

CHICKEN BROTH

You can make delicious broth from nothing more than leftover roasted chicken bones, water, and salt, although it's a great opportunity to use up any wilted vegetables that might be hanging out in your crisper drawer. The recipe is easy: Place the chicken bones in a large stockpot and add enough cold water to nearly cover. An unpeeled yellow onion, chopped in half and added to the pot, will give the broth depth of flavor and impart a lovely golden hue. Now's your chance to add those wilted vegetables; chopped limp celery stalks are perfect for broth, as are slightly wrinkled carrots. Avoid cabbage and its relatives, because their strong flavor is too overpowering. If you like, you can season the broth further by adding a few sprigs of fresh thyme, a small dried hot chile, and a pinch of whole black peppercorns. Bring to a simmer and cook for about 2 hours. Taste for seasoning, adding fine sea salt as needed. Strain the broth through a fine-mesh sieve, discarding the solids. If not using right away, let cool to room temperature before refrigerating or freezing. The broth will keep in an airtight container in the refrigerator for up to 3 days or in the freezer for up to 6 months. (See page 81 for a tip on freezing broth.) Homemade chicken broth is far and away better than the store-bought version. Use it to cook Risotto (page 33), Winter Squash Soup (page 65), and Braised Chicken Legs (page 125). Or try cooking and serving a few Ravioli (page 235) or Shrimp-and-Pork Dumplings (page 243) in a steaming bowl of broth.

Shrimp Summer Bowls with Spicy Peanut Sauce

Serves 2 to 4

These bowls, which are a variation on rice paper–wrapped Vietnamese summer rolls, are ideal picnic food and also make a fabulous packed lunch. You can prepare the various parts ahead of time, assemble each bowl, and add the sauce just before serving. No need for the shrimp to be piping hot; the dish tastes better when served at room temperature, or even slightly cool, especially if it's a particularly hot summer day.

Spicy Peanut Sauce

½ cup (135 g) peanut butter (smooth or crunchy)

¼ cup (60 ml) fresh lime juice (from about 2 limes)

1 teaspoon fish sauce

1 small garlic clove

1 (1-inch/2.5 cm) piece fresh ginger, peeled and finely grated

1 teaspoon brown sugar

1 teaspoon Asian chile sauce, such as sriracha or sambal oelek, plus more if desired

1 tablespoon soy sauce, plus more if desired

3 tablespoons water

Shrimp Summer Bowls

8 ounces (225 g) dried rice noodles (any width)

2 teaspoons toasted sesame oil

1 pound (450 g) medium or large raw shrimp, peeled and deveined

2 teaspoons cornstarch

½ teaspoon fine sea salt

Freshly ground black pepper

1 to 2 tablespoons vegetable oil

1 shallot, thinly sliced

4 to 6 curly lettuce leaves, torn

2 large carrots, thinly sliced (see note)

½ cup (10 g) fresh mint leaves

½ cup (10 g) fresh cilantro leaves

8 large fresh basil leaves

Make the spicy peanut sauce: In a blender or food processor, combine the peanut butter, lime juice, fish sauce, garlic, ginger, brown sugar, chile sauce, soy sauce, and water and blend until smooth. Taste for seasoning, adding more chile sauce and/or soy sauce, if you like. (The sauce can be made ahead and stored in an airtight container in the refrigerator for 1 week.)

Make the shrimp summer bowls: Bring a medium pot of water to a boil.

Place the rice noodles in a large bowl and pour enough boiling water over them to cover. Let stand until just tender, 1 to 3 minutes for ⟶

thin rice vermicelli and up to 10 minutes for flat, wide noodles. Taste a noodle to determine if they're cooked; it should be pliable but not mushy. Drain in a fine-mesh sieve and rinse under cold water to stop the cooking. Return the noodles to the bowl, drizzle the sesame oil over the top, and toss to coat the noodles. (The oil will prevent the noodles from sticking to one another.)

Place the shrimp in a bowl and sprinkle with the cornstarch, salt, and several grinds of black pepper. Use your hands or a spoon to mix well. Heat a large pan over medium-high heat for 1 minute. Swirl in the vegetable oil to coat the pan, then add the shallot and shrimp. Cook, using tongs to flip the shrimp once, until the shallot turns translucent and the shrimp are all just barely opaque, 2 to 3 minutes. Transfer the shrimp and shallot to a bowl.

To assemble the bowls, arrange a bed of lettuce in the bottom of each serving bowl and pile a big handful of noodles on top of the lettuce. Add some carrot, mint, cilantro, and basil, followed by the shrimp and shallot. Spoon some peanut sauce over the top and toss everything together.

An Easy Way to Slice Carrots After you've peeled the carrots, continue using the peeler to create long, thin strips of carrot. It's faster than using a knife and creates pleasantly asymmetrical ribbons.

Fried Fish Tacos

Serves 4

Let's do away with any worries you have about the difficulties of cooking fish and frying foods at home. I promise that making these fish tacos will not take over your entire day, nor will it create the mess you might be imagining. The process is actually quick (plus, there's a fun treat for the cook hidden within the recipe). While you've got the oil hot and the batter mixed, you might as well fry a little more than two servings—leftover pieces of fried fish are delicious on a soft roll with Lime Crema (page 271) and Quick Slaw (page 96).

1 pound (450 g) firm, white-fleshed fish, such as cod, rockfish, halibut, or flounder (see note)

2 quarts (1.9 L) vegetable oil

1 cup (125 g) all-purpose flour

1 teaspoon fine sea salt

1 teaspoon paprika

1 (16-ounce/475 ml) bottle or can of beer

Corn tortillas

Hot Sauce (page 267, or store-bought), for serving

Lime wedges, for serving

Fresh cilantro, for serving

Cut the fish into strips about 1 inch (2.5 cm) wide and somewhere between 2 and 3 inches (5 and 7.5 cm) long. Remove any pinbones using your fingers or small clean pliers. Pat dry.

In a heavy-bottomed pot (such as a Dutch oven), heat the oil over medium-high heat to 350°F (175°C). It will shimmer but shouldn't smoke.

Meanwhile, in a large bowl, whisk together the flour, salt, and paprika. While whisking, gradually add the beer in a slow, steady stream until the batter is a bit thicker than heavy cream. (Any beer left in the bottle or can is the cook's reward.)

To test the temperature of the oil, flick a drop of the batter into the pot. It should float on the surface and sizzle as soon as it meets the oil.

Using your fingers, pick up a piece of fish, dunk it in the beer batter, then carefully place it into the hot oil. Repeat to add a few more pieces to the pot, but be sure not to crowd the pot or they won't brown as nicely. Cook, turning once, until dark golden brown and crisp, about 4 minutes. Using a slotted spoon, transfer the fried fish to a wire rack to cool. Repeat with the remaining fish. ⟶

Warm the tortillas either directly over a flame on the stovetop or in a skillet over medium heat until soft, turning to cook both sides. Place 1 or 2 tortillas per taco on each plate and top with the fried fish. Serve right away, with hot sauce, lime wedges, and cilantro.

Which Fish to Fry? Choose the freshest firm, white-fleshed fish at the market. Thick fillets like cod and rockfish are ideal because they can hold on to more of the delicious crunchy coating.

FOUR TIPS FOR FRYING

1   Take extra care when cooking with very hot oil. Set out every tool and ingredient you'll need before you start heating the oil. You can use metal utensils like tongs, but be aware that they heat up quickly when they come in contact with the hot oil. When you place an ingredient in the frying oil, try to lower it in slowly rather than dropping it from a height of many inches. You don't want to create a cannonball-like splash.

2   If you're cheating and not using quite enough oil—something I've been known to do—the battered pieces of fish will sink to the bottom of the pot and stick there. After a few minutes, you can scrape a wooden spoon along the bottom of the pot, nudging the fish until it releases. It's crucial that you wait until a crust has formed before trying to nudge the fish, because otherwise you'll just tear the coating.

3   When you're left with a small amount of batter in the bowl and the oil is still hot, you might as well fry other foods, like the vegetables languishing in your crisper drawer. Slice dense vegetables (such as sweet potatoes and carrots) into thin rounds and leave light, tender vegetables (such as scallions and mushrooms) in large pieces. Tofu that's been patted dry with paper towels works quite well as a vegetarian substitute for the fish. Fried whole fresh herb leaves are delightful!

4   You can reuse the frying oil to make this recipe again. Let the oil cool completely, then pour it through a funnel lined with a coffee filter into a clean, empty bottle. The fish flavor lingers, so the oil is perfectly fine for frying fish again, but don't use it to fry something sweet like doughnuts.

Setting the Table

Whether you're preparing a casual lunch or hosting a special dinner, take the time to set your table beautifully. This doesn't mean the table setting must be elaborate. An inviting table can be set with only a plate and fork for each person. When you're planning out what needs to be done before guests arrive, add "set the table" to your list and decide who will be in charge of this important job.

This is a comprehensive template for each place setting, but you shouldn't feel pressured to include every single one of these pieces. In fact, I don't think I have ever set a table with them all. Simply leave out any piece you won't need.

PLATE

I've never in my life measured the distance from the edge of the table to the rim of the plate, but in case you're curious, the proper distance is 1 inch (2.5 cm).

NAPKIN

Use any material and pattern you love. Fold the napkin and place it in the center of the plate or to the left of the fork. I'm fond of mismatched napkins on the same table.

FORK(S)

The smaller salad fork should be set to the left of the larger dinner fork. For most meals, a salad fork probably isn't necessary.

KNIFE

One way to remember where the knife is placed is to think about how most people are right-handed. They'll probably feel comfortable cutting with their dominant hand. The sharp edge of the knife faces inward toward the plate for safety reasons.

SPOON(S)

Place a large spoon (for soup or broth) to the right of the knife. Traditionally, the dessertspoon, which is smaller than the soupspoon, goes above the plate, parallel to the edge of the table. It is also perfectly acceptable—and sometimes simpler—to bring any flatware needed for the dessert course to the table when you serve dessert.

GLASSES

The water glass should be placed above and to the right of the plate, and the wineglass slightly behind it.

OTHER ITEMS ON THE TABLE

If you would like to serve the meal family-style, passing platters of food around for everyone to take as much as they wish, make sure to leave space for the platters to rest. Some people may like to add a pinch of salt to their food, so place a tiny dish of flaky sea salt somewhere on the table. For gatherings of eight or more people, put out two salt dishes, one on either end of the table. Fill up and chill a couple of jugs of water and place them on the table, or fill a large pitcher with ice water. It's best to use only unscented candles, because you don't want the smell of a candle to compete with the aromas of the meal.

SIMPLE FLOWER ARRANGING

Flower arrangements should be short enough (or slim enough) that you can see across the table. Use any type of vessel: glass vases, ceramic jugs, jam jars, and water pitchers all work equally well. Stick to muted colors for the vessel to help direct attention to the flowers themselves. A single bloom in a narrow-necked vessel can be visually striking. Several spread out along the length of the table are even more impressive. If combining more than one stem in a vessel, cut some stems shorter than others. The varying height adds a sense of movement to the arrangement and reflects the randomness and beauty of nature. Look around you—in your backyard, along roads, in abandoned lots—and clip foliage, budding branches, and so-called "weeds" like Queen Anne's lace. They are lovely as complementary stems or in a table arrangement all their own. Last, consider nonflower centerpieces. Seasonal fruit in a wide, shallow bowl looks wonderful and, as a bonus, can be eaten! In autumn, try scattering colorful dried leaves down the center of the table like a runner. Evergreen branches, holly, and pinecones are all festive during winter.

Vegetarian Mains

There are many reasons you might want to cook a vegetarian meal at home. Maybe you've chosen one day a week to cook a meatless meal, maybe you splurge for meat only on special occasions for economic reasons, or maybe you eat vegetarian meals every day. Each recipe in this chapter leads to a hearty, satisfying main course that won't leave you missing meat. Some dishes, like Kale-Mushroom Strata and Green Lasagne, are plenty filling on their own, while others, like Winter Squash Soup and Leek and Goat Cheese Tart, pair naturally with a slice of bread or a side salad. In every month of the year, you'll find extraordinary vegetables at the market, ready to be brought into your kitchen and cooked. Seek out those you've never tasted, and don't be surprised if you discover a few new favorites.

Nothing-in-the-Fridge Pasta

Serves 4

Here's a terrific dinner to make after you've come home from a long trip and there is nothing in the fridge. Or when friends stop by and you invite them to stay for an impromptu dinner. As long as you have a decently stocked pantry (see page 19), you'll be good to go.

Fine sea salt

2 tablespoons unsalted butter

3 tablespoons olive oil

5 or 6 garlic cloves, sliced

Red pepper flakes

⅓ cup (45 g) pine nuts (see note)

3 tablespoons capers (see note), rinsed

1 pound (450 g) dried bucatini or any other pasta shape

Freshly grated Parmigiano-Reggiano cheese

Bring a large pot of generously salted water to a boil.

While the water heats up, in a large skillet, melt the butter over medium heat. Once the butter foams, add 2 tablespoons of the olive oil, then the garlic, a pinch or two of red pepper flakes, and ¼ teaspoon salt. Cook, stirring, until the garlic is light golden, 30 seconds to 1 minute. Add the pine nuts and capers and cook, stirring frequently, until the nuts are lightly toasted, about 3 minutes. Remove the pan from the heat.

Once the water is boiling, add the pasta and cook, stirring a few times to prevent sticking, until al dente. (Ignore the instructions on the package because they are almost always wrong. Instead, taste a noodle after 5 minutes, and again every minute thereafter. The pasta is done when it tastes soft but still has a chewy resistance when you bite down. If you cut a noodle, you'll see a tiny speck of white in the center.)

Reserve about 1 cup (240 ml) of the pasta cooking water, then drain the pasta. Transfer the noodles directly to the skillet, set it over medium-high heat, and add about three-quarters of the reserved water and the remaining 1 tablespoon oil. Cook, stirring often, until the sauce coats the noodles, 1 to 2 minutes. There should be a little sauce pooling at the bottom of the skillet; if there is not, add more cooking water and stir well. Serve with Parmigiano on the side for sprinkling.

Substitutions Chopped olives could stand in for the capers. If you don't have pine nuts, substitute walnuts, almonds, or pistachios, or leave the capers and nuts out entirely and call it *pasta aglio e olio* (pasta with garlic and oil).

Miso-Seasoned Tofu and Vegetables

Serves 4 to 6

Miso soup is comforting and nourishing, but it is usually followed by a second course and sometimes even a third because it's not quite filling enough for a whole meal. This dish takes the idea of miso soup and turns it into a main course by packing it to the brim with mushrooms, snow peas, bok choy, and cubes of tofu. Serve with a fork and a spoon.

Steamed Rice

3 cups (720 ml) water

¾ teaspoon fine sea salt

1½ cups (300 g) white rice

Tofu and Vegetables

1 (14-ounce/400 g) block firm tofu

3 cups (720 ml) cold water

1 (6-inch-long/15 cm) piece kombu seaweed

2 tablespoons red miso paste

2 tablespoons neutral-flavored oil, such as grapeseed or canola

1 bunch scallions, cut into 2-inch (5 cm) lengths

1 small dried hot chile, such as Sichuan, stemmed, seeded, and finely chopped, or ¼ teaspoon red pepper flakes (optional)

Fine sea salt

2 cups (150 g) sliced fresh shiitake mushroom caps

2 cups (165 g) snow peas, strings removed

1 large or 2 small baby bok choy, sliced

1 teaspoon toasted sesame oil

4 garlic cloves, thinly sliced

1 (2-inch/5 cm) piece fresh ginger, peeled and finely grated

1 tablespoon soy sauce, plus more if needed

½ cup (30 g) chopped fresh cilantro

Make the steamed rice: In a medium saucepan, bring the water to a boil over high heat. Add the salt and rice. Reduce the heat to low, cover the pot, and cook for 18 minutes. Remove the lid and fluff the rice with a fork.

Meanwhile, make the tofu and vegetables: Place the tofu in a colander in the sink. Set a couple of small but heavy plates or dishes on top of the tofu to weigh it down and press out the excess liquid. Let drain while you prepare the broth.

Combine the cold water and kombu in a medium saucepan and warm over medium heat. Keep an eye on the pan—you want the water to get hot but not boil. When the water is steaming and the seaweed has unraveled and swelled, reduce the heat to low. Fish out and discard the seaweed.

Put the miso in a small bowl, add a ladleful of the seaweed broth, and whisk to break up and dissolve the miso. Pour the loosened miso into the pot with the broth and whisk to combine. Cut the tofu into bite-size cubes and add them to the broth.

Heat a large skillet or wok over high heat for 1 minute. Pour the vegetable oil into the skillet and then add the scallions and chile (if using). Season with ¼ teaspoon salt. Cook, stirring a few times, until the scallions are darkly browned in several places, 3 to 4 minutes. Using tongs, transfer the browned scallions to the broth.

Add the mushrooms and a pinch of salt to the skillet and cook, stirring a few times, until completely tender and browned, about 4 minutes. Transfer the mushrooms to the broth.

Add the snow peas and bok choy and a ladleful of miso broth to the skillet and cook, stirring frequently, until the vegetables turn a bright, vibrant green, 2 to 3 minutes. Transfer them to the broth.

Reduce the heat under the skillet to medium-low. Add the sesame oil, garlic, and ginger and cook, stirring continuously, until the garlic is fragrant and golden, 30 seconds to 1 minute. Remove the skillet from the heat, add the soy sauce, and scrape the garlicky-soy mixture into the broth. Stir well. Taste the broth and add another splash of soy sauce if you'd like it to be saltier.

Serve hot over the steamed rice, with the cilantro scattered on top.

Where to Find Miso and Kombu? You can find miso paste and kombu seaweed in Asian grocery stores, as well as at most health food stores and high-end grocers.

Leek and Goat Cheese Tart

Serves 4

Paired with a Simple Leafy Salad (page 84), this savory tart makes for a lovely dinner at home, but it can also be carried in a picnic basket to the park—it tastes great at room temperature. Or you could cut the baked tart into bite-size squares and serve them hot to a group of guests as an appetizer.

1 sheet frozen puff pastry

3 ounces (85 g) soft goat cheese, crumbled

¼ cup (60 ml) plus 1 tablespoon heavy cream

Fine sea salt and freshly ground black pepper

1 large leek (about ¾ pound/340 g), white and light-green parts only (see note)

1 tablespoon unsalted butter

1 tablespoon olive oil

¼ cup (35 g) pitted Kalamata or other olives, or an assortment (see note)

1 teaspoon fresh marjoram or thyme leaves (optional)

1 large egg

Preheat the oven to 425°F (220°C). Line a baking sheet with parchment paper.

Remove the puff pastry from the freezer and let it defrost for a few minutes. When it has thawed enough to be unfolded, place it on the prepared baking sheet.

In a food processor, combine two-thirds of the goat cheese, ¼ cup (60 ml) of the cream, a pinch of salt, and a few grinds of pepper and process until smooth. (Alternatively, you can blend everything together in a large bowl with a wooden spoon and some vigorous stirring.)

Slice the leek into thin rounds. Drop them into a large bowl of cool water, then swish with your fingers to dislodge any trapped sand or dirt. Let sit for a few minutes; the leek rounds will float and the dirt will sink to the bottom of the bowl.

Meanwhile, in a large skillet, melt the butter with the olive oil over medium-high heat. Using your fingers, lift the leeks out of the bowl (leaving any dirt behind at the bottom of the bowl) and add them to the skillet. Season with ¼ teaspoon salt and a few grinds of pepper. Cook, stirring occasionally, until soft, about 4 minutes. Remove from the heat and let cool slightly. $\longrightarrow$

Use the tip of a small knife to score a border 1 inch (2.5 cm) in from the edge of the puff pastry—be careful not to cut all the way through the pastry. (This edge will puff up in the oven to become the tart's crust.) Spread the goat cheese mixture evenly over the pastry, staying within the border.

Arrange the cooked leeks on top of the cheese, then scatter the olives, marjoram (if using), and remaining crumbles of goat cheese over the top.

Beat the egg with the remaining 1 tablespoon cream. Brush the egg mixture over the exposed pastry border. (You won't need to use all of the egg mixture; sometimes I cook what is left into a tiny bit of scrambled eggs.)

Bake the tart until the crust is puffed and deep golden brown, 15 to 25 minutes. Serve hot straight out of the oven, warm, or at room temperature.

Substitutions Feel free to switch up the toppings to your liking. Purple Kalamata olives make a nice visual contrast to the light-green leek, but you could try wrinkly black oil-cured olives or Castelvetranos, or even substitute capers or marinated bell peppers. If you want to make this with meat, scatter crumbled cooked sausage or bacon on top before baking. During summer, forgo the leeks and substitute thickly sliced tomatoes and a handful of torn fresh herbs.

The Glories of Puff Pastry Many foods are worth making at home, but puff pastry is just not one of them. High-quality store-bought versions abound; they taste great, and they're so convenient. Most recipes call for defrosting frozen puff pastry overnight in the refrigerator, but you don't really need to. It thaws quickly at room temperature. Just give it a few minutes before trying to unfold it; otherwise, it can crack.

Winter Squash Soup with Turmeric and Yogurt

Serves 6

Consider this soup recipe a template. You can follow the same series of adaptable steps without being too concerned about the precise ingredients. Any type of hard-skinned winter squash will do: kabocha, acorn, or butternut. You could even use a combination. You can also choose to switch up the spices. I've included turmeric, a member of the ginger family, because it adds a subtle tang and vibrant pop of color, but you could use a pinch of ground chile for a warming soup. The fresh thyme adds an ever-so-slightly herbal note, but it is optional.

3¾ pounds (1.7 kg) winter squash, such as kabocha, acorn, or butternut

4 tablespoons (60 ml) olive oil

Fine sea salt and freshly ground black pepper

2 tablespoons unsalted butter

1 small yellow onion, chopped

1 carrot, chopped

2 garlic cloves, sliced

Leaves from 3 sprigs fresh thyme (optional)

1 teaspoon ground turmeric

1 quart (960 ml) chicken broth (see page 47) or water

Plain whole-milk yogurt (see note)

Snipped fresh chives or other fresh tender herb leaves, such as cilantro or chervil

Preheat the oven to 400°F (200°C).

Carefully halve the squash lengthwise or widthwise. (If the squash is particularly awkward in its weight distribution and you're worried about cutting into it, you can slice off a thin piece of the peel on one side and then turn the squash so that it rests steadily on the cut side. This will help it stay put and not roll around on your cutting board.) Scoop out and discard the seeds. Place the halves cut-side up on a rimmed baking sheet. Drizzle 2 tablespoons of the oil over the squash and season generously with salt and pepper. Roast until tender when poked with a fork, 45 minutes to 1 hour.

Let the squash cool until you can handle it comfortably. Using a large spoon, scoop the flesh of the squash into a bowl; discard the skins. (The squash can be roasted and scooped ahead of time and stored, covered, in the refrigerator for up to 3 days.) ⟶

Heat a Dutch oven or large pot over medium heat. Add the butter and remaining 2 tablespoons olive oil. When the butter foams, add the onion, carrot, garlic, thyme, turmeric, and ½ teaspoon salt. Cook, stirring often, until the onion softens, about 3 minutes. Stir in the squash and broth. Adjust the heat so the soup simmers, then cook for 10 minutes.

Using an immersion blender, puree the soup directly in the pot until very smooth, or carefully transfer it to a countertop blender and puree. (If using a countertop blender, work in batches and remember to remove the center of the blender lid, then cover the hole with a kitchen towel to avoid steam buildup.) Taste and add another ¼ teaspoon salt (or more), if needed.

To serve, ladle the soup into bowls, swirl a spoonful of yogurt into each, and top with a sprinkling of chives.

Garnishes This soup takes well to all kinds of garnishes. In place of the yogurt, try a drizzle of cream or a dollop of Lime Crema (page 271). Snipped fresh chives look and taste lovely, but so do torn leaves of any fresh tender herb.

Thick-Skinned Squash Winter squash is characterized by its hard, thick skin. Peeling the skin off the squash can be awfully tricky, so opt for roasting the squash until tender, then scooping the meat of the squash out of the skin and into a bowl.

Hearty Tabbouleh with Chickpeas and Feta

Serves 4

If you're searching for a quick-cooking whole grain, look no further than bulgur. Bulgur is one of many names for wheat that has been steamed and then dried and cracked into tiny pieces. (You may also find it sold as "bulgar wheat" or "bulghur"; be sure not to confuse it with cracked wheat, which looks similar but has not been previously steamed and therefore takes longer to cook.) I learned this easy way to cook bulgur from Itamar Srulovich and Sarit Packer of Honey & Co. in London.

1 cup (190 g) fine or coarse bulgur

¼ cup (60 ml) plus 1 tablespoon olive oil

Fine sea salt

¾ cup (180 ml) boiling water

2 garlic cloves

Zest and juice of 1 lemon, plus more as needed

1 bunch flat-leaf or curly parsley, very finely chopped

1 bunch mint, very finely chopped

1 (15-ounce/425 g) can chickpeas, drained and rinsed

2 large tomatoes, finely chopped

3 ounces (85 g) feta cheese

1 teaspoon ground sumac (optional)

In a small bowl, mix together the bulgur, 1 tablespoon of the oil, and ¼ teaspoon salt, stirring until the grains are coated with the oil.

Pour the boiling water over the bulgur and immediately cover the bowl tightly with plastic wrap. Let stand for at least 10 minutes while you prepare the rest of the dish.

Using a mortar and pestle or the back of a large knife, pound the garlic and ½ teaspoon salt to a paste. Transfer the garlic paste to a small bowl and stir in the lemon zest, lemon juice, and remaining ¼ cup (60 ml) oil. (If you used a mortar and pestle, just make the dressing in the mortar.)

Uncover the bulgur and fluff it with a fork. Taste a bite of the bulgur. If it's crunchier than you'd like, cover and let steam for 5 minutes more.

In a large bowl, combine the bulgur, parsley, mint, chickpeas, tomatoes, and garlic dressing. Mix well, then taste. If the tabbouleh tastes a little flat, add another pinch of salt and a squeeze of lemon juice. Crumble the feta over the top, sprinkle with the sumac, if desired, and serve.

Summer-on-a-Platter Salad

Serves 4

This colorful salad celebrates the bounty of ingredients available during the summer. The vegetables in this recipe are only a suggestion. Pay a visit to your local farmers' market and fill your bag with all the beautiful produce that catches your eye.

4 thick slices country-style bread

¼ cup plus 3 tablespoons (105 ml) olive oil, plus more as needed

Fine sea salt

3 large eggs

⅓ cup (80 ml) buttermilk

6 fresh basil leaves, thinly sliced

2 teaspoons apple cider vinegar, plus more if needed

1 large garlic clove

Freshly ground black pepper

1 large head romaine lettuce, chopped

1 pint cherry tomatoes, halved

1 ripe avocado, sliced

½ lemon

¼ cup (35 g) roasted bell peppers (store-bought, or see page 195)

3 Persian cucumbers, thinly sliced

12 Castelvetrano olives, pitted

Tear the bread into bite-size pieces. Heat a large skillet over medium heat. Swirl in 3 tablespoons (45 ml) of the oil and add the bread. Cook, stirring occasionally, until crisp and golden, about 6 minutes. Season with salt and let cool.

Meanwhile, bring a small pot of water to a simmer. Lower the eggs into the water and cook them for exactly 8 minutes. Transfer the eggs to a bowl of ice water, let cool for a few minutes, then peel the eggs.

Combine the buttermilk, basil, and vinegar in a bowl. Using a mortar and pestle or the back of a large knife, pound the garlic and ¼ teaspoon salt to a paste and add it to the bowl. While whisking, slowly pour in the remaining ¼ cup (60 ml) oil. Add a few grinds of pepper, then taste the dressing and add a little more salt and/or vinegar if it tastes flat.

Scatter the lettuce across a large platter. Arrange the tomatoes on one side on top of the lettuce and season them generously with salt and pepper. Fan out the avocado next to the tomatoes and season with salt and a big squeeze of lemon juice. Pile the peppers and cucumbers alongside the avocado and season with salt and a splash of olive oil. Cut the boiled eggs into quarters, place them near the tomatoes, and season with salt and lots of pepper. Finally, scatter the olives over everything. Serve the croutons in a bowl and the dressing on the side so you can add as much of each as you prefer.

Green Lasagne

Serves 6

The traditional recipe for lasagne involves quite a few steps, including making two kinds of sauce (tomato and béchamel) and boiling dried pasta noodles—and that's all before assembling the actual dish. You can streamline the process by using instant, no-boil pasta. No-boil pasta works beautifully in lasagne, softening between the sauce layers but still retaining a nice slightly firm texture at the core of each noodle. Perhaps best of all, using no-boil pasta saves you loads of time and makes what seems like a labor-intensive dish so much easier.

3 tablespoons unsalted butter, plus more for the baking dish

2 tablespoons olive oil

2 large bunches chard, kale, or spinach (about 1½ pounds/680 g), stemmed and coarsely chopped

Fine sea salt

3 tablespoons all-purpose flour

3 cups (720 ml) whole milk

3 garlic cloves, sliced

1 cup (60 g) chopped fresh tender herbs, such as flat-leaf parsley, basil, and/or chives

Freshly ground black pepper

8 ounces (225 g) fresh ricotta cheese

8 ounces (225 g) goat cheese

1 teaspoon finely grated lemon zest

1 pound (450 g) instant (no-boil) lasagna noodles

½ cup (55 g) freshly grated Parmigiano-Reggiano cheese

Preheat the oven to 375°F (190°C). Butter a 9 by 13-inch (23 by 33 cm) baking dish.

Heat a large pan over medium-high heat. Swirl in 1 tablespoon of the oil and pile about half the greens into the pan. Cook, stirring often, until the greens are wilted and vibrantly green, 2 to 3 minutes. Season with ¼ teaspoon salt and transfer to a colander. Return the empty pan to the stove and repeat to cook the remaining greens. Let the greens drain and cool in the colander while you prepare the sauce. Once cooled, squeeze out any excess water.

In a heavy-bottomed saucepan, melt the butter over medium heat. Add the flour and cook, stirring continuously, for 1 minute. Add a splash of the milk to start, then, while whisking continuously, gradually pour in the rest of the milk in a slow, steady stream. Cook, whisking continuously, until thickened, about 5 minutes. Remove the béchamel from the heat and whisk in the garlic, herbs, ¾ teaspoon salt, and lots of pepper. →

In a medium bowl, stir together the ricotta, goat cheese, and lemon zest.

To assemble the lasagne, spread about ½ cup (120 ml) of the béchamel across the bottom of the prepared baking dish. Top with one-quarter of the noodles in a single layer. Spoon about ½ cup (120 ml) of the sauce over the pasta, arrange one-third of the greens over the sauce, and dot one-third of the ricotta mixture on top of the greens. Repeat the process to make two more layers. Arrange the remaining noodles on top, cover with the rest of the béchamel, and scatter the Parmigiano evenly over the béchamel. Cover the dish with aluminum foil. Bake for 20 minutes, then remove the foil and bake until browned and bubbling, about 30 minutes more. Let cool slightly before serving.

How to Make Ahead If you'd like to prepare this dish ahead of time, follow the recipe through to the end, then let the lasagne cool to room temperature before covering it tightly and freezing it. To reheat, allow the lasagne to thaw before warming it, covered with aluminum foil, in a preheated 325°F (160°C) oven until hot in the center, about 45 minutes.

Spring Vegetable Curry with Rice Noodles

Serves 4

Sometimes inviting a group of friends over for a meal can feel like solving a puzzle. One friend eats only gluten-free foods, another is vegan, and a third happens to be on a new dairy-free diet. This spring vegetable curry will satisfy everyone.

Fine sea salt

1½ pounds (680 g) spring vegetables, such as asparagus, young carrots, peas, and/or pea shoots (see note)

1 pound (450 g) fresh or dried rice noodles (any thickness)

2 teaspoons toasted sesame oil

1 lemongrass stalk

3 garlic cloves

½ teaspoon ground turmeric

1 (2-inch/5 cm) piece fresh ginger, peeled and finely grated

1 small hot chile, such as serrano, seeded and thinly sliced

Finely grated zest of 2 limes

1 (13.5-ounce/400 ml) can full-fat coconut milk

Juice of 1 lime, plus more if needed

1 scallion, thinly sliced

Leaves from 4 sprigs fresh Thai basil or regular basil

Bring a large pot of salted water to a boil.

Cut the vegetables into bite-size pieces. Cook the vegetables, one variety at a time, until tender but still pleasantly crunchy in the center, then transfer to a plate and let cool. No need to boil peas and pea shoots; they're already tender. Reserve the cooking water.

Place the rice noodles in a large bowl and pour enough of the hot cooking water over them to cover. Let stand until just tender, 1 to 2 minutes for thin rice vermicelli and up to 10 minutes for flat, wide noodles. Taste a noodle to determine if they're cooked; it should be pliable but not mushy. Drain in a fine-mesh sieve and rinse under cold water to stop the cooking. Transfer the noodles to a bowl, drizzle the sesame oil over the top, and stir to distribute. (The oil will prevent the noodles from sticking to one another.)

Trim off and discard all but the bottom few inches of the lemongrass. Peel away the tough green layers until you reach the softer purple-white interior. Chop very finely and place in a small bowl. Using a mortar and pestle or the back of a large knife, pound the garlic to a paste. Add it to the bowl with the lemongrass. Stir in the turmeric, ginger, half the chile, and the lime zest. ⟶

Heat a large pan over medium-high heat. Open the can of coconut milk and spoon the thick, creamy part that has risen to the top into the pan. Add the lemongrass mixture and cook, stirring often, for a few minutes. Pour in the remaining coconut milk, then fill the can about halfway with water and pour that into the pan as well. Add the vegetables and cook, stirring, until heated through, 1 to 2 minutes. Add ½ teaspoon salt and half the lime juice, stir well, and taste. Season with more salt and lime juice, if needed.

Serve the curry and rice noodles together in a shallow bowl, garnished with the scallion and basil. Place the remaining sliced chile in a small dish on the table for adding a little extra spice.

Substitutions Don't worry if it isn't springtime where you are—any kind of vegetable will work in this recipe. Try sweet potatoes during the fall, and broccoli and cauliflower florets during the winter. If the vegetable isn't tender enough to eat raw, you'll want to boil it until tender before mixing it into the curry sauce.

Kale-Mushroom Strata

Serves 6

Strata is a fantastic dish to serve guests because it can be assembled ahead of time. Also, the recipe can be easily adapted to suit almost any meal. Are half of your guests vegetarians? Split this into two smaller baking dishes, leaving one vegetarian and tucking pieces of cooked sausage into the other. Feel free to vary the vegetables and cheeses to your liking; just make sure to use a meltable cheese (such as cheddar, mozzarella, Monterey Jack, provolone, or Fontina) in place of the Gruyère. The grated Parmigiano-Reggiano sprinkled across the top of the strata bakes into a browned and crispy crust, so make sure not to skip it.

1 (1-pound/450 g) bunch lacinato kale (dinosaur or Tuscan kale)

2 tablespoons olive oil

1 yellow onion, sliced

½ pound (225 g) mushrooms, sliced

1 tablespoon fresh thyme leaves

Fine sea salt and freshly ground black pepper

Unsalted butter

1 (1-pound/450 g) day-old loaf of bread

1 cup (110 g) freshly grated Gruyère, Comté, or Emmental cheese

8 large eggs

2 cups (480 ml) whole milk

½ cup (55 g) freshly grated Parmigiano-Reggiano cheese

Stem the kale and tear the leaves into 3-inch (7.5 cm) pieces.

Heat a large pan over medium-high heat. Swirl in the olive oil and add the onion. Cook, stirring occasionally, until softened, about 3 minutes. Add the mushrooms and thyme and cook, stirring two or three times, until the mushrooms are browned in a few places, 3 to 4 minutes. Stir in the kale. Cook for a couple of minutes more, until the kale wilts. Season with ½ teaspoon salt and lots of pepper. Remove from the heat and let cool.

Butter a 9 by 13-inch (23 by 33 cm) baking dish.

Cut the bread into 1-inch (2.5 cm) cubes, leaving the crusts on, and spread the cubes across the bottom of the prepared baking dish. Scatter the Gruyère evenly over the bread. Using tongs, transfer the kale-mushroom mixture to the dish. Poke the tip of the tongs around the dish in a few places, forcing some of the mushrooms and kale toward the bottom and distributing them evenly.

In a large bowl, whisk together the eggs, milk, ¾ teaspoon salt, and lots of black pepper. Pour the eggs into the baking dish and press down with a spatula. Sprinkle the Parmigiano evenly over the top. Cover with aluminum foil and refrigerate for at least 1 hour or, ideally, overnight.

When you're ready to bake the strata, remove it from the refrigerator and let stand at room temperature for 30 minutes. Preheat the oven to 350°F (175°C).

Bake the strata, covered, for 20 minutes. Remove the foil and bake until golden brown on top, 30 to 40 minutes. Let cool for 5 minutes before serving.

Variation

BRUNCH STRATA

To make a brunch-worthy strata, leave out the kale and mushrooms. Cook about six slices of bacon or ham in a pan over medium heat until crisp. Transfer to a paper towel to drain, then add the bacon or ham to the dish before pouring in the egg-milk mixture. Instead of Gruyère, use cheddar cheese. Scatter three thinly sliced scallions over the top of the strata before baking.

Organization Strategies for Storing Food

Keeping a tidy, organized kitchen will help you become better cooks because you'll know where everything is and you'll be inspired to use your ingredients. As a general rule, store like with like: Keep all the spices in one place and all the nuts in another. Bonus points for putting the most frequently used groups of ingredients front and center. For example, if you love baking, make sure the flour and sugar are easily accessible. Here are a few more strategies and tips for organizing your pantry, refrigerator, and freezer.

PANTRY

By storing bulk goods in clear glass jars, you'll be able to see exactly what's inside and how much you have on hand at any given time. Half-gallon jars are about the right size for flour, sugar, and rice. Quart jars are better for foods used less often, like dried fruit, although this will depend on your personal preferences. Choose widemouthed jars, as these are easier to fit a sponge inside when it comes time to clean them. If you've ever spent time in a restaurant kitchen, you've probably noticed how most chefs label containers of food, using a permanent marker to write the name and date on a piece of masking tape and then sticking that tape on the outside of the container. Try employing this practical solution at home.

REFRIGERATOR

Think of your refrigerator as a miniature world, with its own microclimates. The coldest place is at the bottom along the back wall. This is where you should keep highly perishable dairy items like milk and cream. Butter doesn't need to be quite as chilled and can be stored in the door, where there's often a designated space for it. Store eggs in the door, too, if they fit. The best way to keep fresh herbs perky is to rinse them as soon as you bring them into your kitchen. Dry them thoroughly (a salad spinner works well) and then wrap a clean kitchen towel around the herbs to catch any remaining drops of water. Stash the herbs, wrapped in the towel, in your crisper drawer. The herbs will stay fresh there for days. Mushrooms prefer a cool, humid environment, so store them in a paper bag in the refrigerator.

FREEZER

Because foods tend to hang out in the freezer for longer than in the refrigerator, it's important to clearly label everything. Also, some frozen foods look similar to one another, and you wouldn't want to make the regrettable mistake of confusing pork lard

for vanilla buttercream. To maximize space (and create more room for ice cream!), freeze broths and soups in plastic bags set on a flat surface like a baking sheet. Once frozen, stand the bags upright like books on a shelf. Fresh summer berries freeze remarkably well and are wonderful to have around during the doldrums of winter, when you might crave a Blackberry Crumble (page 155) or a breakfast parfait (see page 182). Spread cleaned berries in a single layer on a rimmed baking sheet and freeze until solid, then transfer them to a plastic bag and label it. Nuts are more perishable than many people realize—their oils turn rancid if exposed to too much sunlight or heat. It's best to store nuts in tightly sealed bags in the freezer.

Sides

You might think that side dishes are secondary to the main course, but this doesn't account for the game-changing role a side can play as part of a meal. When considering which side dish to cook, imagine how it will taste with the main dish in a single bite. Sometimes like goes well with like—a spoonful of buttery polenta is wonderful with meltingly tender braised chicken—but other times you may want to emphasize contrasting textures or temperatures. The bracing cold crunch of slaw nicely balances rich carnitas in a taco. Occasionally, you may crave a particular side dish even more than its usual main-dish partner. If you feel this way, try inverting the proportions of the side to the main. A huge Caesar salad with a few slices of leftover roasted chicken makes a quick and terrific dinner, as does an overflowing platter of sautéed Broccolini paired with a more modest serving of steaming-hot shrimp-and-pork dumplings.

Simple Leafy Salad and Mustard Vinaigrette

Serves 2 to 4

The most important step in making an excellent salad is thoroughly drying the greens. Any droplets of water clinging to them will dilute the salad dressing and prevent the dressing from coating them. As the saying goes, oil and water do not mix. Keep this idea in mind when making salads of all kinds but especially when preparing a simple salad such as this one. *Pictured with Sicilian Fennel-Citrus Salad on page 92.*

1 head butter lettuce or other tender-leafed lettuce

½ cup (10 g) fresh tender herb leaves, such as flat-leaf parsley, basil, mint, chervil, or dill, or a combination

1 small garlic clove

Fine sea salt

2 tablespoons fresh lemon juice, plus more as needed

1 teaspoon red wine vinegar

Freshly ground black pepper

Dijon mustard

3 tablespoons olive oil

Trim the bottom of the head of lettuce and discard any bruised outer leaves. Rinse the individual lettuce leaves and the herbs by first swishing them in a large bowl of cold water or gently washing in a colander under running water. Dry the lettuce and herbs thoroughly in a salad spinner. (If you feel like the salad spinner isn't doing the job, try dividing the greens into two batches. Sometimes having less in the spinner helps the leaves to shake off every last droplet of water.) Line a very large bowl with a clean kitchen towel and place the clean lettuce and herbs in the bowl. If the lettuce leaves and herbs are large, tear them into smaller pieces. Refrigerate, uncovered, while you make the dressing. (The low humidity inside the fridge will dry the greens a little further.)

Using a mortar and pestle or the back of a large knife, pound the garlic and a pinch of salt to a smooth paste. Transfer to a small bowl and stir in the lemon juice, vinegar, ¼ teaspoon salt, and several grinds of pepper. (If you used a mortar and pestle, just make the dressing in the mortar.) Dip the tines of a clean fork into the mustard jar. When you lift the fork, a small amount of mustard should cling to the tines. Dunk the fork into the lemon juice mixture and stir to incorporate. Pour in the olive oil and stir until emulsified. Taste the dressing—if it is too tart, add a little more olive oil; if it tastes oilier than you prefer, add another squeeze of lemon juice.

Remove the kitchen towel from the bowl of clean lettuce and herbs. Season the greens with a pinch or two of salt and a few grinds of pepper, then add about half the dressing. Use your hands to gently toss the salad until the leaves are evenly coated—your hands are the best tool for tossing salads because unlike salad tongs, they won't bruise or tear the leaves, and also because you can literally feel the moment when all the leaves are evenly dressed. Taste a leaf and add more dressing if you like. (Store any leftover dressing in an airtight container in the refrigerator for up to 3 days.) Serve right away on individual plates or a large platter.

A Tip for Measuring Mustard Measuring mustard—especially in tiny amounts—can be a messy affair, so I came up with a useful trick: Dip a clean fork into a jar of mustard; when you lift out the fork, there will be a small amount of mustard stuck to the tines (if it seems like more than you want, just tap the fork on the edge of the jar to release some). Use this fork to stir the dressing and incorporate the mustard all at once.

Salad for a Winter's Night

Serves 4 to 6

Instead of everyday leafy greens, this salad is mainly composed of Belgian endive and radicchio, two vegetables in the chicory family. They are the ideal shape to act like little scoops and catch the toasted walnuts and dabs of soft, creamy blue cheese. Don't forget to take the cheese out of the refrigerator about an hour before making this salad—you want it to be at room temperature so that it has a smooth texture and tastes its best.

1 cup (115 g) walnuts

1 large or 2 small Belgian endives

1 large head radicchio

1 large apple

1 garlic clove

1 anchovy, rinsed

Fine sea salt

2 tablespoons fresh lemon juice

2 teaspoons red wine vinegar

3 tablespoons olive oil

4 ounces (115 g) soft, creamy blue cheese, such as Cambozola or Saint Agur, at room temperature

Freshly ground black pepper

Flaky sea salt

Preheat the oven to 350°F (175°C).

Spread the walnuts out on a baking sheet and toast in the oven until golden brown inside, about 10 minutes. (Cut one in half to check.)

Meanwhile, trim the base of the endive and gently separate the individual leaves, trimming a bit more off the base as needed to detach the inner leaves. Separate the radicchio into individual leaves and, if the leaves are quite large, tear them into smaller pieces. Place the endive and radicchio in a very large bowl.

Slice the apple thinly, discarding the core, and add to the bowl. Add the toasted walnuts to the bowl.

Using a mortar and pestle, pound the garlic, anchovy, and a pinch of fine salt to a smooth paste. Stir in the lemon juice, vinegar, olive oil, and ¼ teaspoon fine salt.

Drizzle most of the dressing over the salad. Toss gently with your hands until the leaves are evenly coated. Taste and add more dressing, if you like. Transfer the salad to a serving platter. Tuck little dabs of the blue cheese in and around the leaves. Season with lots of pepper and a pinch of flaky salt. Serve right away.

Caesar Salad

Serves 4 to 6

There are three steps to putting together a classic Caesar salad: (1) Rinse and dry the lettuce, (2) make the dressing, and (3) toast the croutons. You needn't go in that order, though. If you're in a hurry, divide and conquer—one of you can be in charge of the dressing, which involves making aioli, while the other prepares the lettuce and croutons. Or, if you're cooking at a more leisurely pace, you can work as a team. No matter what, don't toss everything together until just before serving, because a Caesar salad tastes best immediately after it has been dressed. You could even toss the salad at the table.

1 large head romaine lettuce

3 or 4 anchovies, rinsed

¾ cup Aioli (page 273)

½ lemon

Freshly ground black pepper

¼ cup (30 g) freshly shaved Parmigiano-Reggiano cheese, plus more for sprinkling

4 thick slices country-style bread

3 tablespoons olive oil

Flaky sea salt

Chop the romaine into bite-size pieces, rinse, and dry thoroughly. (Any water clinging to the leaves will dilute the dressing and make the salad soggy. For tips on drying lettuce, see page 84.)

Using a mortar and pestle or the back of a large knife, pound the anchovies to a smooth paste. Stir the anchovy paste into the aioli along with a big squeeze of lemon juice, lots of pepper, and the Parmigiano. Taste and adjust the seasoning, adding more lemon juice as needed.

Tear the bread into irregularly shaped 1½-inch (4 cm) pieces. Heat a large pan over medium-high heat. Add the oil and the bread pieces. Cook, stirring often, until golden brown in a few places and crisp on the outside, 6 to 8 minutes. Season the croutons with ¼ teaspoon salt. Let cool.

Place the romaine in a very large bowl. Add about half the dressing. Using your hands, gently toss until the leaves are evenly coated. Add the croutons and pour a little more dressing over them. Toss again. Add the remaining dressing, if you'd like. Top with more pepper, Parmigiano, and a pinch of salt. Serve the salad immediately on a platter or in a wide, shallow bowl.

Pomelo-Mango Salad

Serves 4 to 6

Could it be that the more difficult a fruit is to eat, the more delicious it tastes? Or is it just that after prying back layers and gently coaxing out the good parts, we find the reward so sweet and well deserved? In this salad, two of those difficult-to-prepare fruits come together on one platter. Because the fruits demand your attention, the dressing ought to be simple, and this one is.

⅓ cup (50 g) peanuts or cashews, coarsely chopped

1 pomelo

2 mangoes

2 tablespoons fresh lime juice

Pinch of brown sugar

1 fresh red Thai or Fresno chile, seeded and finely chopped (optional)

2 tablespoons olive oil

¼ cup (5 g) fresh mint leaves, torn into small pieces

Flaky sea salt

Preheat the oven to 350°F (175°C).

Spread the peanuts out on a baking sheet and toast in the oven until golden brown inside, 8 to 10 minutes. (Cut one in half to check.)

Meanwhile, cut off the bottom and top of the pomelo and peel away the rind and spongy white pith. Use your fingers to gently remove the fruit from the surrounding membrane, and place the fruit segments on a serving platter.

Mangoes have an oblong pit in the center. To cut around it, stand a mango up on its stem end and cut down on one side, just beyond where you think the pit might be. If the knife meets resistance, you may be cutting too close to the pit; move the knife away from the center of the fruit, cutting around the pit. Repeat with the other sides, then with the second mango. Cut each side piece in a crosshatch pattern, cutting through the fruit but not all the way through the peel. Press the peel side to invert the mango piece so that the little squares pop out like a porcupine's quills. Cut the fruit away from the peel. You may be able to cut a bit more fruit from the pit, or just snack on the center pieces, gnawing around the pit as if it were a corncob. Add the mango to the platter.

In a small bowl, use a fork to stir together the lime juice, brown sugar, chile (if using), and olive oil. Drizzle the dressing over the fruit. Scatter the toasted peanuts and mint over the top. Sprinkle with a pinch or two of salt before serving.

Sicilian Fennel-Citrus Salad

Serves 4 to 6

This recipe teaches two useful cooking techniques. The first one is how to cut a citrus fruit into segments. After cutting off the peel and white pith, squeeze the last drops of juice from those cut pieces and use it to make a quick salad dressing. The second technique is helpful not just for this recipe but for all recipes that require you to pit olives: Press the heel of your hand straight down on an olive and its pit will slip right out. If you're pitting a whole mess of olives, place them on a kitchen towel, fold the towel over the olives, and press down on each olive one at a time or use a rolling pin to get them all in one swift motion. The towel contains the juices that would otherwise squirt out at you. *Pictured with Simple Leafy Salad and Mustard Vinaigrette (page 84).*

1 large fennel bulb

1 Cara Cara orange

3 small blood oranges

Olive oil

Fine sea salt

5 oil-cured black olives

7 Castelvetrano olives

Flaky sea salt

Ground Aleppo pepper

Cut off the leafy top of the fennel, reserving a few fronds for garnish, and trim the base. Cut the bulb in half from top to bottom, through the base. Set each half cut-side down on a cutting board and slice as thinly as possible.

Using an extremely sharp knife, cut off the top and bottom of the Cara Cara orange. Set the orange on one cut side so that it doesn't roll around. Place the blade of your knife at the top of the orange and cut down, tracing the curved line of the fruit, to remove a section of the peel and white pith. Rotate the orange and continue cutting away the peel and pith until you've removed it all. Go back and trim any pith still clinging to the fruit. Slice the orange crosswise into thin rounds, discarding any seeds. Repeat with the blood oranges.

Squeeze the pieces of peel and pith that you cut off, capturing the juice in a small bowl. There should be 1 to 2 tablespoons of juice. Add about the same amount of olive oil and a pinch of fine salt and stir with a fork to combine. →

Arrange the sliced fennel and oranges beautifully on a serving platter.

Use the heel of your palm to press down on each olive—the pit will slip out. (Don't worry if the olives get a little smashed in the process of pitting them. Some olives cling to their pits more than others.) Scatter the pitted olives over the fennel and oranges and garnish the salad with the reserved fennel fronds. Give the dressing another stir, then drizzle it over the salad. Sprinkle with 2 pinches of flaky salt and 2 pinches of Aleppo pepper. Serve immediately or refrigerate, covered, for up to 4 hours.

Variation

GRAPEFRUIT AND OTHER CITRUS

This salad looks best when made with a combination of citrus fruits. You can substitute 1 ruby red grapefruit for the Cara Cara orange, or try using other citrus fruits (such as Oro Blanco grapefruit, Meyer lemon, and pomelo) in place of the blood oranges. For citrus fruits with thick white piths (like some large grapefruits), you may want to cut the fruit into individual segments according to the technique on the preceding page. If using pomelo, follow the technique on page 90.

Quick Slaw

Serves 4 to 6

This recipe is endlessly adaptable and rather forgiving of omissions—even if you leave out the fennel bulb, it will still taste great. I like the way the olive oil coats the cabbage ribbons without obscuring their delightful crunch and clean flavor. The result is quite different from a mayonnaise-laden slaw, which too often disappoints. *Pictured with Money-in-the-Bank Breaded Chicken on page 29.*

1 small red cabbage

1 fennel bulb (optional)

Fine sea salt

1 bunch flat-leaf parsley

1 bunch cilantro

1 lemon, halved

2 limes, halved

4 to 6 tablespoons (60 to 90 ml) olive oil

Freshly ground black pepper

Rinse the cabbage and pull off any limp exterior leaves. Cut in half lengthwise, through the core. Using the tip of your knife, cut out the core. If the cabbage halves seem too big to manage, cut into quarters. Using a very sharp knife (or a mandoline), slice the cabbage as thinly as possible into long, wavy ribbons and place in a large bowl.

If using the fennel, trim the stalks and fronds and cut the bulb into quarters lengthwise, through the flat bottom. Slice each quarter as thinly as possible and place in the bowl with the cabbage. Add a few big pinches of salt, then use your hands to toss well.

Cut off the thicker parsley and cilantro stems, but don't worry about getting rid of the thin, tender branching stems in the top half of the bunches. Give the herbs a quick chop and add them to the bowl.

Add the juice of 1 lemon half and 1 whole lime. Use your hands to toss well. Drizzle in 3 to 4 tablespoons of the olive oil. Toss once again, then taste a bite of the slaw. If you'd like it to be zingier, add more lemon juice and lime juice. If it tastes a bit too tart, add the remaining 1 to 2 tablespoons olive oil. Mix in lots of pepper and season with salt. Serve.

Store any leftovers, covered, in the refrigerator for up to 2 days. The slaw will lose its crunch with time, but even softened slaw is great slaw.

What Else to Serve? This slaw can be made at any time of year, and it comes together in the time it would take you to cook Money-in-the-Bank Breaded Chicken (page 27) or fry some fish for tacos (see page 51).

Creamy Polenta or Grits

Serves 6

There's a cloud of confusion surrounding polenta and grits. Are they the same? Well, no, not exactly, although they are both made from coarsely ground corn. Traditional Italian polenta is milled from a class of corn called flint corn, whereas traditional grits from the American South are milled from dent corn. The good news is, both polenta and grits can be cooked in the same manner—slowly, over low heat, until creamy.

2 cups (325 g) coarse stone-ground cornmeal

2 quarts (1.9 L) water

2 teaspoons fine sea salt

4 tablespoons (½ stick/55 g) unsalted butter

⅓ cup (35 g) freshly grated Parmigiano-Reggiano cheese (optional)

Combine the cornmeal and water in a heavy-bottomed pot. Stir well, then leave the mixture alone for 1 minute. Using a fine-mesh sieve or a tea strainer, skim off any chaff floating on the surface.

Bring to a boil over medium-high heat, stirring continuously with a wooden spoon until the first bubbles appear and the cornmeal unites with the water, 10 minutes or more (although it is tempting to skip the constant stirring, it really is important, or the corn will stick to the pot and burn). Reduce the heat to the lowest setting, cover the pot, and cook until tender and creamy. Every 15 minutes or so, uncover the pot and give the polenta a stir. The total cooking time varies greatly, ranging anywhere from 30 minutes to 2 hours, depending on the cornmeal. Taste to know when it's smooth and no longer crunchy and gritty. If it gets too thick, you can always add a splash of hot water. If it tastes done but you want it to have a thicker consistency, just remove the lid and cook over medium-low heat, stirring often, until some of the water evaporates and the polenta thickens.

When the polenta is done cooking, stir in the salt, butter, and Parmigiano (if using). Serve piping hot.

Store any leftovers, covered, in the refrigerator for up to 3 days. As it cools, the polenta will solidify. To reheat, you can slice it and panfry it in a little butter, or you can slowly warm it in a pot with a splash of water to loosen it up.

What Else to Serve? Polenta and grits are wonderful topped with a fried egg.

Ancho Black Beans

Serves 6

Cooking a pot of beans is not a speedy process. Part of the wonder of dried beans is their ability to be stored at room temperature for years without deteriorating much. So is it any surprise that they need a little coaxing to return to their full glory? Beans take time, but they don't require your constant attention. You can prepare another part of the meal, or read the newspaper, or shake up a cocktail or two (see pages 115 to 119). Despite this recipe's title, the ancho chile, which is in fact a dried poblano, isn't absolutely necessary. The beans will still taste great without it, so don't worry if you can't find one.

2 cups (1 pound/450 g) dried black beans

1 yellow onion

2 garlic cloves

1 ancho chile (see headnote)

1 sprig of oregano (optional)

2 tablespoons olive oil, plus more for drizzling if desired

Fine sea salt

Place the beans in a large, heavy-bottomed pot. Add enough water to cover the beans by 1 to 2 inches (2.5 to 5 cm). Cut the onion in half, peel away the papery layers, and drop the two halves into the pot. Smash the garlic cloves with the flat side of a large knife, discard the peels, and add the cloves to the pot. Add the ancho chile, oregano (if using), and olive oil.

Bring the water to a boil and cook for 10 minutes, then reduce the heat so that the liquid barely simmers. Partially cover the pot and cook until the beans are completely soft all the way through, 1 hour 30 minutes to 2 hours total, depending on the age of the beans. Every so often, uncover the pot, give the beans a stir, and check the water level. If the beans are poking out, add more hot water to submerge them. When the beans are almost done, stir in 1 teaspoon salt, wait a few minutes, then taste a bean and a sip of broth. Add more salt to taste, knowing that only the broth will taste salty at first and then the beans will slowly absorb the salt. Fish out and discard the onion halves and ancho chile (but don't worry about finding the garlic). It's not a big deal if a few onion pieces remain in the pot.

Bean broth is delicious—don't discard it! Serve the hot beans in a shallow pool of their broth, topped with a drizzle of olive oil, if you like. Store any uneaten beans in their broth in an airtight container in the refrigerator for up to 4 days.

Green Rice with Preserved Lemon

Serves 4 to 6

Most recipes for cooking rice involve steaming the grains in a precise amount of water. It's difficult to remember if the correct ratio is 1:1 or 1:2 or something else entirely. Instead of worrying about how much water to add, try this: Boil the rice in plenty of salted water and then drain it, just like you would if you were cooking pasta.

Fine sea salt

3 cups (600 g) medium-grain brown rice

1 large bunch flat-leaf parsley

1 large bunch dill

½ Preserved Lemon (page 246, or store-bought)

3 garlic cloves

Juice of 2 lemons

½ cup (120 ml) olive oil

Freshly ground black pepper

Bring a large pot of salted water to a boil. Add the rice and cook at a boil until tender but not mushy, 30 to 40 minutes.

Meanwhile, use a large knife to cut off and discard the thick stems of the parsley and dill. Don't worry about the thinner, branching stems near the top of the bunch—they're tender and delicious. Use the dull edge of a small knife to scrape out the squishy flesh of the preserved lemon; discard the flesh, reserving the peel. Combine the herbs and preserved lemon peel in a food processor or blender. Add the garlic, lemon juice, olive oil, and ½ teaspoon salt and blend until smooth. (Alternatively, for a more rustic-looking green rice, you can chop the herbs, preserved lemon, and garlic, then mix in the lemon juice, olive oil, and salt.)

When the rice is done, drain it and return it to the pot it was cooked in. Stir in the green sauce and season with more salt and pepper. Serve warm.

For Other Types of Grains This technique works well for brown rice and other whole grains such as barley and farro but can be a bit too vigorous for white rice. (If cooking white rice, follow the recipe on page 60.)

What Else to Serve? Serve this bright, herby rice under a piece of sautéed fish or alongside Roasted Chicken (page 45) with a Simple Leafy Salad (page 84).

Food Processor Potato Gratin

Serves 8 to 10

Of course, you don't *need* a food processor to make this potato gratin, but using one will significantly speed up the process. Most basic models come with a few different blade attachments, including a slicing blade that makes quick work of both onions and potatoes, as well as a shredding disc that can be used to grate cheese. You'll be sliding a fully assembled gratin into the oven before you know it.

2 tablespoons unsalted butter, plus more for the baking dish

2 cups (480 ml) heavy cream

2 bay leaves

4 sprigs thyme

3 garlic cloves, sliced

Fine sea salt and freshly ground black pepper

1 large yellow onion, halved

3½ pounds (1.6 kg) russet or Yukon Gold potatoes, peeled

6 ounces (170 g) Gruyère, Comté, or Emmental cheese (with no rind)

4 ounces (115 g) Parmigiano-Reggiano cheese (with no rind)

Preheat the oven to 400°F (200°C). Generously butter a 9 by 13-inch (23 by 33 cm) baking dish.

In a small saucepan, combine the cream, bay leaves, thyme, garlic, 1 teaspoon salt, and several grinds of pepper and bring to a boil. Remove from the heat, cover, and let steep while you prepare the onion and potatoes.

Using a food processor fitted with the slicing blade, slice the onion. Transfer it to a bowl. Using the same blade, slice the potatoes. Transfer them to the prepared baking dish, spreading evenly. Switch the food processor blade to the shredding disc and use it to grate the Gruyère. Scatter the Gruyère over the potatoes. Use the food processor to grate the Parmigiano, then transfer the Parmigiano to a bowl and set aside.

In a large skillet, melt the butter over medium heat. Add the onion and ¼ teaspoon salt. Cook, stirring occasionally, until the onion is golden in a few places, about 6 minutes. Scrape into the baking dish, using the spoon to spread the onion evenly over the cheese and potatoes.

Uncover the cream, fish out and discard the bay leaves (don't worry about the thyme, unless the sprigs are quite woody), then pour the cream into the baking dish. Cover the dish with aluminum foil. Bake for 45 minutes, then remove the foil, scatter the Parmigiano over the top, and bake until bubbling and browned, about 20 minutes.

Roasted Whole Cauliflower with Crisp Pancetta

Serves 4 to 6

A roasted whole cauliflower looks impressive and tastes great. To encourage browning and caramelization, many recipes call for rubbing the cauliflower with olive oil, but draping thin slices of pancetta over the vegetable works even better. As the pancetta cooks in the hot oven, it crisps and browns, slowly basting the cauliflower with its flavorful fat. You'll want to trim the tough parts of the cauliflower, but be careful not to be too overzealous or the vegetable will break into pieces. Don't worry if that does happen; just reassemble them into a cauliflower-shaped mound. It'll still taste fantastic!

1 large cauliflower

7 or 8 very thin slices of pancetta (about 2 ounces/55 g)

2 garlic cloves

Fine sea salt

2 cups (40 g) fresh tender herbs, such as dill, mint, cilantro, or basil

1 tablespoon red wine vinegar

2 tablespoons fresh lemon juice

6 tablespoons (90 ml) olive oil

Freshly ground black pepper

Preheat the oven to 400°F (200°C).

Trim any cauliflower leaves and use the tip of a small knife to carefully cut out the base of the core without causing the vegetable to break into pieces. Set the cauliflower right-side up in a baking dish. Drape the pancetta slices over the cauliflower, overlapping them slightly so they stay put. Roast until the pancetta is crisp and browned and the cauliflower is tender all the way through when poked with the tip of a small knife, about 1 hour.

Meanwhile, using a mortar and pestle, pound the garlic and ½ teaspoon salt to a smooth paste. Add the herbs, a handful at a time, and pound to incorporate them. (Alternatively, use the back of a large knife to mash the garlic and salt to a paste, transfer to a bowl, then finely chop the herbs and mix them into the garlic paste.) Stir in the vinegar, lemon juice, and olive oil. Season with pepper and more salt as needed.

Transfer the roasted cauliflower to a serving dish. Spoon the herb sauce over the top.

Sautéed Broccolini with Garlic and Chile

Serves 4 to 6

The combination of lemon, garlic, and chile makes this side dish feel Mediterranean, but you can leave out the lemon juice and olive oil and instead drizzle a little soy sauce over the cooked Broccolini for a dish that pairs well with all manner of Asian food, especially Shrimp-and-Pork Dumplings (page 243). On a busy weeknight, you might even cook the Broccolini with soy sauce, but pick up dumplings from your favorite takeout restaurant.

Fine sea salt

3 bunches Broccolini (sometimes called baby broccoli; about 1½ pounds/680 g)

2 tablespoons unsalted butter

1 tablespoon olive oil

3 or 4 garlic cloves, thinly sliced

¼ teaspoon red pepper flakes

½ lemon

Bring a large pot of salted water to a boil. Cut off and discard the bottom 1 inch (2.5 cm) or so of the Broccolini stems. Add the Broccolini to the boiling water and cook until the thickest part of the stem is tender but not mushy, about 5 minutes. Drain.

In a large skillet, melt the butter with the olive oil over medium heat. Add the garlic and red pepper flakes and cook, stirring, until fragrant, 1 minute. Add the drained Broccolini and ¼ teaspoon salt. Toss well and cook for another minute.

Immediately transfer to a platter (if you leave the Broccolini in the skillet, it will continue cooking and lose its fresh green color), squeeze some lemon juice over the top, and serve.

Home Bar

Drinks at home can take many celebratory forms: a cocktail sipped in the early evening, a favorite bottle of wine enjoyed with dinner, a digestif after a holiday meal. Even when there isn't an obvious festive occasion, sharing a couple of drinks together still feels romantic and special. In the same way that you set yourselves up for success in the kitchen, you'll also want to build a strong foundation for your home bar. Start with the essential tools and ingredients, and add to your collection slowly over time. You can raise your glasses often *and* stay within your budget. Cheers to that!

COCKTAILS

A well-stocked home bar, with all the necessary tools, ingredients, and glassware, will allow you to prepare two perfect cocktails for each other or a whole tray of frosty drinks for guests at a moment's notice. Here's everything you need to know to get started mixing cocktails.

ESSENTIAL BAR TOOLS

First, you'll need a tool to open bottles. There are many fancy gadgets on the market, but the simplest ones are the best. Choose a waiter's friend–style corkscrew that has a built-in bottle opener. This classic tool has endured the test of time for a reason: It's sturdy, small enough to fit in a pocket, and so beautifully crafted you'll feel proud displaying it. Next up, a jigger is helpful for accurate measuring. Most jiggers are composed of two opposing metal cones; one side holds ½ ounce (15 ml), while the other holds 1 ounce (30 ml). If you don't have a jigger, use measuring spoons and remember that 2 tablespoons equals 1 ounce. For shaken drinks, you're going to need a cocktail shaker. You may have seen bartenders using what looks like a metal tin shoved onto a pint glass. This is known as a Boston shaker, and it is the professional standard. At home, a regular metal cocktail shaker with a built-in strainer on top works just fine and eliminates the need for additional straining tools. Last, although not absolutely essential, a classic wooden muddler comes in handy for mashing fruits, herbs, and sugar cubes. You can use a wooden spoon in a pinch.

There's some overlap between bar tools and kitchen tools. Reach for a peeler to remove strips of citrus zest for twists. In your freezer, keep two full ice cube trays at the ready. Some cocktail connoisseurs prefer a single large ice cube for a drink served on the rocks because it melts more slowly than many smaller cubes, keeping the drink colder and less diluted. If you like, you can buy large (usually 2-inch/5 cm square) ice cube molds.

STOCKING YOUR BAR

Liquors come in such a wide range of styles and prices, it can be difficult to know where to start. Best to begin by choosing two or three different types that are key components in cocktails you love. For example, to make the recipes in this book, buy a bottle each of whiskey, gin, and tequila. At the liquor store, tell an employee that you'll be using the alcohol primarily in mixed drinks but would like something good enough to sip on its own. He or she will direct you to a high-quality yet affordably priced option. Once you have stocked the ingredients for your favorite cocktail, it's okay to wait before buying more alcohol. Give yourself some time to learn more about your preferences. Friends who come over for dinner might bring you a gift of their favorite liquor, and you may find your home bar collection slowly growing over time. When you're ready to return to the liquor store, consider picking up a sweet red vermouth and a dry white vermouth, which will expand the number of cocktails you can make. Until you know which vermouth is your favorite, select a 375 ml bottle, modest in size and price. Remember that vermouth,

unlike most spirits, does spoil and should be stored in the fridge after you've opened it, where it will keep for up to 1 month. Next, explore the fascinating world of aperitifs and digestifs. Often bitter-tasting, these spirits are meant to either begin or conclude a meal. They whet the appetite, aid in digestion, and can be enjoyed on their own or mixed into cocktails. As you become a more ambitious home bartender, consider keeping vodka, rum, and brandy on hand. Curiously, quality vodka is prized for its pure, clean taste—in other words, its lack of flavor. For this reason, choose an economical vodka to which you will add layers of complexity. Finally, flourishes can make all the difference in cocktails; bitters (your first purchase could be a classic like Angostura, or try making your own—see page 255) contribute subtlety, and cocktail cherries (see Resources, page 294) are, well, the cherry on top.

GLASSWARE

Although there are uniquely shaped glasses for all kinds of cocktails, you really need only two types: a set of short, heavy-bottomed rocks glasses (sometimes called old-fashioned glasses) and a set of tall, slender highball glasses (sometimes called Collins glasses). In general, the former holds a stiff drink served neat (meaning made without ice or a mixer) or a cocktail served over ice like a Negroni (page 117), while the latter better accommodates drinks that are lighter in alcohol and often fizzy, such as Palomas (page 115). I don't mind sipping a cocktail served "up"—that is, chilled but served without ice—in a short rocks glass, but the proper vessel is a third type called a coupe. These can be particularly beautiful, with their shallow bowls balancing atop thin stems, like blossoms, and would make a spectacular gift. Coupes are also elegant glasses for serving champagne.

DESIGNATE A HOUSE COCKTAIL

Knowing how to precisely make a cocktail by heart is a real skill, and it takes practice to get right. At first, focus your efforts by mastering just one cocktail. Call it your "house cocktail," or name it if you want, and stick to it. Ours is the whiskey sour (see page 116). I'm not sure we've perfected it quite yet, but we've made many improvements and had a whole lot of fun in the process.

HOW TO OFFER SOMEONE A DRINK

It's easy to feel stressed by the notion that you're expected to be able to prepare any kind of cocktail under the sun for your guests. As in, *What if I offer to make James a drink and he asks for an extra-dry dirty martini and I don't know how to make it?* Don't get bogged down by these thoughts. Instead, before your guests arrive, plan one cocktail you'd like to serve. Gather and prepare the ingredients, but wait to mix the drinks until your lucky friends have set foot in your home. Cocktails, like omelets, are best made *à la minute*. Simply ask James, "Can I interest you in a [cocktail you've chosen ahead of time]?" Either he will respond with "No, thank you," or he'll be delighted to accept. He'll be even more delighted when you hand him a frosted glass with something delicious inside. If your party is large enough that you or your partner cannot prepare drinks one or two at a time for guests, make it easier on yourselves and stir together a batch of Negroni for a Crowd (page 117).

WINE

Great wine enhances any meal, but selecting a bottle of wine can be intimidating. It sometimes feels like you have to be an expert to decode the jargon on many labels. Here are a few basics to help you feel more confident choosing, opening, and storing wine.

PAIRING WINE WITH FOOD

Forget any rules you've heard about pairing red wine with meat and white wine with fish; just drink what you love, and talk to your partner about which wines taste best with your favorite dishes.

HOW TO OPEN SPARKLING WINE

Part of the excitement of uncorking a bottle of bubbly is the tiny terror you feel. How far is the cork going to shoot? Will the wine surge up and cascade out of the bottle? To alleviate your worries without ruining the fun, follow these steps:

1 Never open a bottle of sparkling wine that has been recently shaken. The pressure inside will be too strong and you'll lose some of the wine when it bubbles up and out of the bottle.
2 Remove the metal cage and foil that often surround the cork.
3 Hold the bottle at a 45-degree angle, and make sure the cork is not pointed at anyone's face or anything easily breakable.
4 Wrap your hand around the cork, thumb on top. As slowly as you can manage, twist the cork up, allowing the pressure inside the bottle to naturally push it out. You'll hear it pop open, and you'll feel the loose cork in your hand.

Unless you're too nervous, share the experience of uncorking the bottle with your guests. It's such a celebratory moment, and everyone enjoys hearing that anticipated *pop!* Remember to pour a small amount of sparkling wine into each glass, then go back around and top them off once the foaming subsides.

STORING WINE

A cork must be properly hydrated in order to do its job. If it dries out, it could fail and allow too much air into the bottle. For this reason, make sure you lay each bottle of wine on its side. Store your wine in a dark, cool place, like in a basement or on a low bookshelf, far away from the stove and heat-emitting fridge. Recork any opened bottles and keep them in the refrigerator. Even better, pour the wine into a smaller vessel like a clean half bottle or a jar, filling it all the way to the top, then close it tightly to keep out as much air as possible. The wine will taste slightly different but still good over the following three days or so. After that, the flavor can teeter on the edge of vinegary.

BEER

You may think you know beer, but consider it again. Like wine, beer can be complex, nuanced, and food-friendly. In recent years, the explosion of small-scale craft breweries has meant that brewers are experimenting with novel techniques and coming up with new styles of beer, all in an effort to distinguish themselves from the pack. There are so many terrific beers out there to try. Here are a few things to keep in mind when deciding which beer to choose.

BEER 101

It takes only four ingredients to make beer: water, malted barley, yeast, and hops. Broadly, beer can be divided into two main styles: ale and lager. Ales are made with top-fermenting yeasts and fermented between 65°F and 75°F (18°C and 24°C), while lagers are made with bottom-fermenting yeasts and fermented at cooler temperatures, between 45°F and 55°F (7°C and 13°C).

SERVING BEER

Remember to chill beer in the refrigerator at least overnight, if not longer, before your party. You want it to be decidedly cold. Sometimes it's nice to say, "There's beer in the fridge. Help yourself." But other times, especially if some guests might not be comfortable rummaging around in your refrigerator, you might consider asking each person upon arrival if he or she would like a beer. If the answer is yes, grab the beer for them, open it, and offer it with an empty glass.

When Company Comes Over

This chapter starts with drinks because that is exactly what you should do first when company comes over. Putting a beverage in a guest's hand is a lovely way to make him or her feel welcome while you finish up any last-minute preparations. For breakfast and brunch, simply ask, "Coffee or tea?" (See page 204 for tips on preparing both.) Or, if you're feeling festive, you can offer guests Bloody Marys. Midday, most people will be happy with a tall glass of ice water, though you might consider having another option like iced tea, or maybe a tray of sparkling, barely boozy Palomas. In the evening, when we all relish the thought of a little bite before dinner, make sure to offer both a beverage and something small and salty like *gougères*. By greeting your guests with a drink and an enticing first bite, you'll naturally create a warm, convivial atmosphere and a little more time, setting yourselves up to host in style and with ease.

Palomas

Serves 6

Icy Palomas are wonderfully thirst-quenching, and they come together easily on a lazy afternoon when friends drop by to catch up. If there's no grapefruit syrup in your home, don't worry—just leave it out and use store-bought grapefruit soda or blood orange soda in place of the sparkling water. You can add as much soda or sparkling water as you like. If you prefer a slightly stronger drink, add only 2 ounces (¼ cup/60 ml) or so and consider serving the cocktail without ice cubes in a chilled short glass, like a coupe. For a less strong drink, top each tall glass with about 4 ounces (½ cup/120 ml) soda or sparkling water. *Pictured with Mixed Citrus Whiskey Sours (left; page 116).*

Ice cubes

1 grapefruit

8 to 10 limes

3 ounces (6 tablespoons/90 ml) grapefruit syrup (page 282; see headnote)

9 ounces (1 cup plus 2 tablespoons/270 ml) blanco or reposado tequila

Sparkling water

Fill six glasses with ice cubes. Using a small knife or a vegetable peeler, cut 6 long, narrow strips of grapefruit peel and 6 strips of lime peel, pressing the blade lightly to remove the peel while avoiding the white pith. Twist the peels into curlicues over the glasses, then drop one peel from each citrus fruit into each glass. Place the glasses in the freezer to chill while you make the cocktails.

Squeeze the limes and measure their juice; you'll need 6 ounces (¾ cup/180 ml) total. Working in batches of two servings at a time (unless you have a very large cocktail shaker), combine 1 ounce (2 tablespoons/30 ml) grapefruit syrup, 2 ounces (¼ cup/60 ml) lime juice, 3 ounces (6 tablespoons/90 ml) tequila, and a handful of ice cubes in a cocktail shaker. Shake until well chilled, about 20 seconds. Strain into two of the chilled glasses. Top each with as much sparkling water as you like, and serve immediately. Repeat twice to make four more cocktails.

What Else to Serve? Palomas go very well with Prosciutto and Ripe Fruit (page 212), a Simple Leafy Salad (page 84), or a spread of Sardines, Baguette, and Lemon (page 223).

Mixed Citrus Whiskey Sours

Serves 6

If you don't already have a favorite cocktail, you're in luck. The whiskey sour is a prime candidate. Nicely balanced between tart and sweet, it's an easy one to love. You'll need to plan ahead and make a simple syrup, which must cool to room temperature before it can be successfully incorporated into cocktails. Once you've made the syrup, however, you can store it in the refrigerator for up to a month. *Pictured with Palomas on page 114.*

Citrus Syrup

1 cup (240 ml) fresh juice from a combination of citrus fruits, such as lemon, orange, and grapefruit

1 cup (200 g) granulated sugar, or 1 cup packed (215 g) brown sugar

Cocktail

Ice cubes

2 large or 4 small citrus fruits, such as lemon, orange, and/or grapefruit

9 ounces (1 cup plus 2 tablespoons/270 ml) whiskey

Sparkling water

6 cocktail cherries (see Resources, page 294; optional)

Make the citrus syrup: In a small saucepan, combine the citrus juice and sugar and bring to a simmer, stirring until the sugar dissolves. Transfer the citrus syrup to a glass jar and let cool to room temperature. (The syrup can be stored in the jar, tightly sealed, in the refrigerator for up to 1 month.)

Make the cocktail: Fill six short glasses with ice cubes and place in the freezer to chill while you prepare the cocktails. Using a small knife or a vegetable peeler, remove 6 strips of citrus peel from the fruits, pressing the blade lightly to remove the peel while avoiding the white pith. Set the strips aside. Squeeze the citrus juice; you'll need 3 ounces (6 tablespoons/90 ml) total.

Working in batches of two servings at a time (unless you have a very large cocktail shaker), combine 3 ounces (6 tablespoons/90 ml) whiskey, 1 ounce (2 tablespoons/30 ml) fresh citrus juice, 1 ounce (2 tablespoons/30 ml) citrus syrup, and a handful of ice cubes in a cocktail shaker. Shake well. Strain into two of the chilled glasses. Top each with a splash of sparkling water and add a cherry, if desired. Holding 1 citrus strip over each glass, twist it, then drop it into the glass. Serve. Repeat twice to make four more cocktails.

Negroni for a Crowd

Serves 8

The recipe for a classic Negroni couldn't be easier to remember: For each drink, stir together an ounce each of gin, Campari, and sweet red vermouth. Serve over ice and garnish with an orange twist. A Negroni makes a fine cocktail to serve to a bunch of friends and family because scaling up the recipe involves only simple math, and better still, the ingredients can be combined well ahead of time, then doled out into individual glasses.

8 ounces (1 cup/240 ml) gin

8 ounces (1 cup/240 ml) Campari or other red bitter aperitif, such as Contratto

8 ounces (1 cup/240 ml) sweet red vermouth

Ice cubes

2 oranges

Pour the gin, Campari, and vermouth into a large glass jar or jug. Cover and chill in the refrigerator until ready to serve.

Fill eight short glasses with ice cubes. Using a small knife or vegetable peeler, cut 8 long, narrow strips of orange peel, pressing the blade lightly to remove the peel while avoiding the white pith. Twist the peels into curlicues over the glasses, then drop one into each glass. Pour in the chilled alcohol mixture, dividing it evenly among the glasses, and serve. ⟶

Which Alcohol to Buy? I love Terroir Gin (distilled by St. George Spirits in Alameda, California) for its evocative aromatics: coastal sage, California bay laurel, and Douglas fir. For excellent sweet red vermouth, try Bruto Americano, also by St. George Spirits, or Carpano Antica Formula, a robust, dark, and not overly sweet option.

Variations

NEGRONI SBAGLIATO

Made famous by Bar Basso in Milan, the Negroni *sbagliato* (meaning "mistaken Negroni") is a delightful bubbly variation: Just leave out the gin and top off each glass with prosecco.

AMERICANO

To make an Americano instead of a Negroni, leave out the gin and top off each glass with sparkling water.

BOULEVARDIER

Substitute whiskey for the gin. Serve neat (without ice cubes) in a chilled glass.

WHITE NEGRONI

Use gentian-based Suze instead of Campari, and Lillet Blanc in place of the sweet red vermouth. Serve neat or over ice. Some people prefer a White Negroni made with a little more gin and a little less Suze, so feel free to play around with the amounts until you've found your favorite ratio.

Manchego-Paprika Gougères

Serves 6

The French cheese puffs known as *gougères* are a crowd-pleaser. Try serving them warm with very cold sparkling wine.

½ cup (120 ml) whole milk

½ cup (120 ml) plus 1 teaspoon water

6 tablespoons (¾ stick/85 g) unsalted butter

Fine sea salt

1 cup (125 g) all-purpose flour

5 large eggs

1 teaspoon sweet paprika

1 cup (110 g) grated Manchego cheese

Preheat the oven to 400°F (200°C). Line two baking sheets with parchment paper and place them in the freezer or refrigerator to chill.

Heat a large saucepan over medium heat. Add the milk, ½ cup (120 ml) of the water, the butter, and ½ teaspoon salt. Once the butter has melted completely, add the flour and stir vigorously with a wooden spoon until a soft dough forms. Cook, stirring continuously, until the dough dries out a bit and pulls away from the pan, about 3 minutes. Transfer to a large bowl and let cool for a few minutes.

Crack 1 egg into the bowl, then vigorously stir with the wooden spoon to incorporate. Add 3 more eggs, one at a time, beating thoroughly after each addition. Don't worry if the batter looks lumpy at first; just keep beating and it will become smooth. Stir in the paprika and three-quarters of the Manchego.

Using two spoons, scoop and place about 9 walnut-size mounds of batter on each baking sheet (for a total of 18 gougères), leaving 2 inches (5 cm) of space between each one. (You can use a piping bag to form perfectly shaped balls, but I actually adore the charm of slightly misshapen gougères.)

In a small bowl, beat the remaining egg with the remaining 1 teaspoon water and a pinch of salt and brush over the top and sides of the gougères. Sprinkle the gougères with the remaining Manchego. Bake for 10 minutes, reverse the position of the two baking sheets, then bake for 15 minutes more. Turn the oven off and open the oven door. Using a sharp knife, pierce each gougère to let some steam escape. Prop the oven door open with a wooden spoon and leave the gougères to cool until just warm. (This will help prevent deflated gougères—they should be crisp on the outside and hollow on the inside.) Serve warm.

Buckwheat Blini

Serves 8 to 12

Buckwheat flour gives these light, yeasted pancakes an earthy flavor. They're smaller than regular pancakes but are cooked the same way and can be made ahead. *Pictured with Manchego-Paprika Gougères (page 120).*

½ cup plus ⅓ cup (200 ml) whole milk

1½ teaspoons active dry yeast

Pinch of sugar

½ cup (60 g) all-purpose flour

⅓ cup (40 g) buckwheat flour

½ teaspoon fine sea salt

2 tablespoons unsalted butter, melted, plus more for the pan

2 large eggs

Crème fraîche (store-bought, or see page 271 and leave out the lime)

1 bunch dill, cut into small sprigs

Smoked salmon, torn into pieces

Salmon roe (*ikura*)

In a small saucepan, warm ½ cup (120 ml) of the milk to no hotter than body temperature (about 100°F/37°C). Pour the warmed milk into a small bowl or measuring cup and stir in the yeast and sugar. Cover and set aside until tiny bubbles form on the surface of the yeast mixture, about 5 minutes. (If the yeast doesn't foam at all, toss it out and start again with new yeast.)

In a medium bowl, whisk together the all-purpose flour, buckwheat flour, and salt. Add the yeast mixture to the bowl along with the remaining ⅓ cup (80 ml) milk and the melted butter. Whisk until smooth. Cover and let rise in a warm place until puffy, about 1 hour.

Separate the egg yolks from the whites. Stir the yolks to break them up, then stir them into the risen batter. Whisk the whites until they hold soft peaks, then gently fold them into the batter.

Heat a large skillet over medium heat. Coat the skillet with a small amount of butter. Drop the batter by small spoonfuls into the hot skillet. Flip each pancake as soon as its surface is covered in bubbles, about 45 seconds. Cook on the second side until browned, 30 seconds or so. Repeat to cook the remaining blini, adding butter to the pan as necessary between batches. (The cooked blini can be stored, covered, in the refrigerator for up to 2 days.)

Just before serving, arrange the blini on a platter. Dollop a little crème fraîche on top of each one. Top some blini with a sprig of dill, place smoked salmon on some, and spoon salmon roe on a select few.

Braised Chicken Legs with Green Olives and Lime Gremolata

Serves 4

There's a culinary rule that I am breaking in this recipe: Traditionally, wine is used in a braising liquid, but I use sherry vinegar instead. One day I was braising chicken and didn't have any wine. I *did* have vinegar, so I just diluted it with water and used it in place of the wine. In the end, I loved how the finished braise tasted more dynamic and zingy than usual. It goes to show that most recipes can be successfully modified to use the ingredients you have on hand—and you might even prefer the results.

4 bone-in, skin-on chicken legs (thigh and drumstick together)

Fine sea salt and freshly ground black pepper

3 tablespoons olive oil

1 large yellow onion, sliced

6 garlic cloves: 4 sliced, 2 finely chopped

¼ cup (60 ml) sherry vinegar, plus more if needed

¾ cup (180 ml) water

6 sprigs fresh thyme

1 tomato, quartered

½ cup (70 g) pitted Castelvetrano olives

2½ cups (600 ml) chicken broth (see page 47)

Zest of 3 limes

½ bunch flat-leaf parsley, finely chopped

Pat the chicken dry—it must be completely dry to brown properly. Generously season with salt and pepper on all sides.

Heat a Dutch oven over medium-high heat for 1 minute. Add the oil and the chicken legs, skin-side down. Cook, without moving the chicken, until dark golden brown, 9 to 12 minutes. Flip and cook on the other side for a few more minutes, until browned. (The chicken will not be cooked all the way through yet.) Transfer the chicken to a plate.

Reduce the heat under the Dutch oven to medium. Add the onion and cook, stirring, until golden in a few places, about 3 minutes. Add the sliced garlic and cook, stirring often, for 1 minute. Pour in the vinegar and water and use a wooden spoon to scrape up any browned bits stuck to the bottom of the pot. Return the chicken legs to the pot, skin-side up. Tuck the thyme, tomato, and olives around the chicken. Pour in enough broth to come three-quarters of the way up the sides of the chicken legs (just the dark golden brown skin should be poking out ➞

of the broth—you may not need to use all of the broth). Bring the liquid to a simmer, cover the pot with the lid, reduce the heat to low, and cook until the chicken is very tender, about 45 minutes.

Carefully pour the braising liquid into a bowl. (It's okay if you don't get every last drop.) Set aside for about 5 minutes to allow the fat to rise to the surface, then use a spoon to skim off the fat. Taste a spoonful of the liquid. If it tastes a little flat, add a pinch of salt and a splash of vinegar. Return the braising liquid to the pot, reuniting it with the chicken, and keep warm over low heat.

The chicken skin will have lost its crispness during the braise. If you want, you can recrisp it by placing just the chicken legs under the broiler for a few minutes. Afterward, return them to the pot.

Just before serving, in a small bowl, stir together the lime zest, parsley, and remaining finely chopped garlic for the gremolata.

To serve, place 1 chicken leg in each of four shallow bowls, spoon some braising liquid and olives around the chicken, and sprinkle the gremolata over the chicken.

Not-So-Traditional Gremolata Gremolata is a mixture of finely chopped lemon zest, garlic, and parsley. Sprinkled over braised meat, it enlivens all the flavors and adds a pop of freshness. Swapping lime for the lemon might not be traditional, but I love the way lime works with the green olives in this dish. In addition to their matching colors, the two ingredients also have complementary verdant flavors.

How to Thicken the Sauce If you'd like the sauce that's served to be thicker and more like gravy, cook 1 tablespoon butter and 1 tablespoon all-purpose flour in a small saucepan over medium heat, stirring continuously for 2 minutes, then pour in the skimmed braising liquid, bring to a simmer, and cook until thickened.

Seafood Stew with Saffron Broth

Serves 6

The rhythm of this recipe works out nicely. You can make the aioli while the seafood broth simmers. You'll also have time to prepare toast. Make lots of it by placing bread slices on a baking sheet, drizzling olive oil over them, and toasting in a preheated 350°F (175°C) oven until golden brown. As soon as the toasts come out of the oven, rub them with a clove of raw, peeled garlic. Keep the toast warm while you finish making the stew, then serve them together and enjoy every spoonful—the leftovers don't reheat well.

1 small fennel bulb

6 cups (1.4 L) water

1 cup (240 ml) white wine

1½ pounds (680 g) fish bones, 1 whole fish head, or shrimp shells (see note)

2 garlic cloves, smashed

4 sprigs fresh thyme

Fine sea salt

1 leek, white and light-green parts only

2 pinches of saffron threads

¾ cup Aioli (page 273)

1 pound (450 g) skinless firm, white-fleshed fish, such as ling cod or halibut, cut into 1½-inch (4 cm) pieces

1 pound (450 g) large raw shrimp, peeled (save the shells for the broth) and deveined

1 pound (450 g) mussels, scrubbed and debearded, any broken or open mussels discarded

Cut off the fennel fronds, chop finely, and reserve for garnishing. Slice the fennel bulb.

In a large pot, combine the sliced fennel, water, wine, fish bones, garlic, thyme, and 1 teaspoon salt. Bring to a boil over medium-high heat.

Slice the leek into thin rounds. Drop them into a large bowl of cool water, then swish with your fingers to dislodge any trapped sand or dirt. Let sit for a few minutes; the leek rounds will float and the dirt will sink to the bottom of the bowl. Using your fingers, lift the leeks out of the bowl (leaving any dirt behind at the bottom of the bowl) and transfer them to the pot.

Once the liquid in the pot boils, reduce the heat so that it simmers gently. Skim off and discard the white foam that floats to the surface— the bobbing leek slices make this step tricky, so don't worry too →

much about skimming off every bit of foam; just get what you can. Cook the broth until full flavored, 30 to 40 minutes.

Meanwhile, using your fingertips, crumble the saffron threads and add them to the aioli. Stir well. Set aside at room temperature while you finish making the stew.

When the broth is done, strain it through a fine-mesh sieve, pressing on the vegetables and bones to squeeze out as much flavor as possible, then discard the solids. Rinse out the pot, then pour the strained broth back into it. At this point, get everything else you'll need ready, but wait to proceed with the recipe until your guests arrive. From here on out, it's a quick few steps till dinner is served.

Bring the broth to just under a simmer—steaming hot but with no bubbles. (It may not look like a ton of liquid, but don't worry, you want the broth to be concentrated and flavorful.) Add the fish, shrimp, and mussels. Cover the pot and cook until the fish pieces are opaque, the shrimp are pink, and the mussels open, about 5 minutes. Remove the pot from the heat. Using a slotted spoon, transfer the seafood to warm shallow serving bowls, making sure each serving has some of each type of seafood. Discard any unopened mussels.

Ladle about ½ cup (120 ml) of the broth into the saffron aioli and whisk until combined, then, while whisking continuously, gradually add the warmed aioli to the broth left in the pot. Cook over low heat, stirring continuously, until slightly thickened, about 3 minutes. Taste the broth and add more salt, if needed. It should be salty enough to pleasantly remind you of the sea. Ladle the broth into the bowls, garnish with the reserved fennel fronds, and serve right away.

Homemade Seafood Broth Making seafood broth is just like making chicken broth (see page 47), only with fish bones. When you buy the fish, shrimp, and mussels for this stew, ask if you can also buy bones, ideally from white-fleshed fish. Most fishmongers will give them away or sell them at a very low price. If they don't have any fish bones, they might have whole fish heads. One salmon head will be enough. And if neither fish bones nor a fish head is available, just use the shells from the shrimp. Shells may not weigh quite as much as bones, but they are surprisingly flavorful.

Whole Side of Salmon and Herb Sauce

Serves 8

My tried-and-true method for cooking a whole side of salmon is roasting it at a low temperature. There's no need to worry about undercooking or overcooking because the fish cooks slowly, gently coasting into the perfect range of doneness.

Salmon

3 large handfuls of fresh herb sprigs, such as rosemary (optional)

1 whole skin-on side of salmon (about 3 pounds/1.4 kg)

Olive oil

Fine sea salt and freshly ground black pepper

Herb Sauce

3 garlic cloves

2 tablespoons capers, rinsed

2 bunches flat-leaf parsley, tough bottom stems trimmed

2 tablespoons red wine vinegar, plus more if needed

Zest and juice of 1 lemon

1 teaspoon fine sea salt, plus more if needed

Freshly ground black pepper

¾ cup (180 ml) olive oil

Make the salmon: Preheat the oven to 250°F (120°C).

Mound the fresh herb sprigs (if using) on a baking sheet and spread them out into a fluffy bed about the same size and shape as the salmon. Place the salmon, skin-side down, over the herbs. Drizzle about 2 tablespoons oil over the fish and season generously with salt and pepper. Bake until just cooked in the center, 20 to 40 minutes, depending on thickness. To test for doneness, poke a fork into the thickest part of the fish and twist—if the salmon flakes apart, it's done. You can also try sticking the handle of a wooden spoon underneath the fillet and gently lifting—look for the salmon to flake apart.

Make the herb sauce: In a food processor, combine the garlic, capers, parsley, vinegar, lemon zest, lemon juice, salt, and lots of pepper and process until the parsley is finely chopped. You may need to stop the machine and scrape down the sides a couple of times. Add the olive oil and process to combine. Taste, adding more salt if needed. If the sauce tastes oilier than you'd like, stir in another splash of vinegar.

Serve the salmon warm or chilled, with the herb sauce on the side.

Meatball Sandwiches

Serves 8

It's such fun to invite a bunch of friends over to your home for a casual daytime party. People can come and go, stopping in to enjoy a bite to eat, and there's no pressure to serve a huge hot meal to everyone all at once. Put out an assortment of dishes that taste best at room temperature or can be easily warmed. Don't worry if you don't have enough chairs for everyone. Your friends can sit on the carpet or on a cushion, and they won't mind, as long as there are delicious things to eat. These meatball sandwiches are a fantastic option because they can be assembled ahead and kept warm in the oven.

1 large yellow onion

5 garlic cloves, minced

½ cup (120 ml) whole milk, plus more as needed

1¼ cups (135 g) bread crumbs, plus more as needed

3 large eggs

1 bunch flat-leaf parsley, tough stems trimmed

Leaves from 5 sprigs fresh oregano

1 pound (450 g) ground pork

1 pound (450 g) ground beef (80% lean or less)

½ cup (55 g) freshly grated Parmigiano-Reggiano or Pecorino Romano cheese

½ teaspoon red pepper flakes

Fine sea salt and freshly ground black pepper

Olive oil

3 tablespoons unsalted butter

1 (28-ounce/795 g) can whole peeled tomatoes, with their juices

Handful of fresh basil leaves

2 loaves Italian bread, each at least 12 inches (30 cm) long

2 cups (480 ml) Herb Sauce (see page 131), or 7 ounces (200 g) store-bought pesto

4 cups loosely packed (about 6 ounces/170 g) arugula

Preheat the oven to 450°F (230°C). Line two rimmed baking sheets with parchment paper.

Grate the onion on the large holes of a box grater into a large bowl. This is a surefire way to make a person cry—accept my apologies in advance—but it really is the best way to cut the onion to the right size. You can use a knife and very finely mince it, if you prefer. Using a mortar and pestle or the back of a large knife, pound the garlic to a paste. Add the garlic paste to the bowl with the onion along with the milk, bread crumbs, and eggs. Mix well, then set aside to rest for a few minutes. →

Meanwhile, finely chop the parsley and oregano leaves. Add them to the bowl along with the pork, beef, cheese, red pepper flakes, 1½ teaspoons salt, and lots of black pepper. Use your hands to mix everything together, squeezing the meat until it feels slightly sticky—a thorough mix will help the meatballs stay together, but if you knead for too long, the meatballs will be tough. As soon as the meat starts feeling tacky, you're ready for the next step.

Grab a small handful of the meat mixture and form it into a patty. Heat a small pan over medium heat. Add a little oil to the pan and cook the patty, flipping once, until cooked through. Taste. If the test patty could use a bit more salt, add a couple of pinches to the meat mixture in the bowl. If the test patty crumbles apart, use your hands to squeeze and mix the meat mixture for another minute or two. On the other hand, if the test patty seems too tough, soak a handful of bread crumbs in a generous splash of milk, then very gently mix into the meat mixture.

Once you feel satisfied with the flavor and texture, shape the meat mixture into balls about the size of small apricots and place them on the prepared baking sheets. Roast, rotating the baking sheets halfway through, until the meatballs are browned on the undersides, about 20 minutes.

Meanwhile, in a large pot, melt the butter over medium-high heat. Add the tomatoes with their juices. Stir in a few pinches of salt. Fill the tomato can about halfway with water and pour it into the pot. Toss in the basil. Bring to a simmer and cook, stirring occasionally to break up the tomatoes, until thickened, about 15 minutes. Add the roasted meatballs and simmer for 5 minutes or so more.

Cut the bread loaves in half lengthwise. Spread the herb sauce over the bottom halves of the loaves and arrange the arugula over the sauce. Spoon the meatballs and as much of their sauce as you want over the arugula. (If you're serving right away, lots of tomato sauce is great, but if you're preparing these sandwiches ahead of time, it's better to add only a small amount of sauce.) Place the top halves of the loaves over the meatballs. (At this point, you can wrap the sandwiches tightly with aluminum foil and keep warm in a 250°F/120°C oven until ready to serve.)

Cut the sandwiches crosswise into pieces as large or small as you like. Try serving the whole sandwiches, cut into individual pieces, on a long platter or wooden board, in the center of your table. Your friends can reach in and grab the piece nearest to them.

Sunday Roast Beef and Horseradish Cream

Serves 8 to 10

Having friends and family over for roast beef doesn't have to break the bank. If it's a casual Sunday night gathering, turn to the lean, economical cuts. They aren't marbled with as much fat and must be carefully cooked in a way that leads to juicy, tender meat. In this recipe, you'll use a technique known as the reverse-sear. First, you roast the meat slowly at a low temperature, then you finish by quickly searing the outside of the roast, which both seals in the juices and creates a nice brown crust. The meat inside remains perfectly pink from edge to edge. This roast beef partners very well with Food Processor Potato Gratin (page 102) and Salad for a Winter's Night (page 87).

Fine sea salt and freshly ground black pepper

3 pounds (1.4 kg) boneless beef top round, top sirloin, or eye of round

Olive oil

5 garlic cloves

Leaves from 2 sprigs fresh rosemary, finely chopped

2 tablespoons unsalted butter

¾ cup (180 ml) heavy cream

¾ cup (180 g) crème fraîche (store-bought, or see page 271 and leave out the lime)

3 ounces (85 g) fresh horseradish, peeled and finely grated

1 bunch chives, chopped

Juice of 1 lemon

Place the meat on a plate and sprinkle 2 teaspoons salt and 2 teaspoons pepper evenly over all sides of the meat. Cover with plastic wrap and refrigerate for at least 4 hours or, ideally, overnight.

When you're ready to roast the meat, preheat the oven to 250°F (120°C).

Uncover the meat and place it on a wire rack set inside a rimmed baking sheet. Rub oil over the top and sides. Roast until a thermometer inserted into the thickest part of the meat reaches 115°F (46°C), 1 hour 15 minutes to 2 hours.

When the beef is getting close to done, use a mortar and pestle or the back of a large knife to pound the garlic and a pinch of salt to a smooth paste. Stir the rosemary into the paste.

Once the beef is done, remove it from the oven. Heat a large cast-iron skillet over high heat for 1 minute. Add the butter, and once it melts, use tongs to transfer the beef to the skillet. Sear, turning the ⟶

roast with the tongs, until browned on all sides, 45 seconds to 1 minute per side. Transfer the roast beef to a serving platter. At this point, the internal temperature will have risen to around 125°F (52°C) and the meat will be medium-rare. Spread the rosemary-garlic paste across the top and sides of the roast beef. Tent loosely with aluminum foil and let rest for at least 20 minutes.

Meanwhile, in a large bowl using a whisk or handheld mixer, or in the bowl of a stand mixer fitted with the whisk attachment, whip the cream until it holds soft peaks. Gently fold in the crème fraîche, horseradish, chives, and lemon juice. Season with salt and pepper. (The horseradish cream can be made ahead and stored in an airtight container in the refrigerator for up to 1 week.)

Slice the roast beef across the grain as thinly as possible. Serve with the horseradish cream on the side.

When Is It Done? The best way to ensure that the roast is cooked to the proper doneness is to check its internal temperature with a thermometer. You can purchase a decent probe-style version for around twenty dollars, or invest in a fancier model that has a countertop digital display connected by a cord to an oven-safe thermometer.

Cut Across the Grain Because these cuts of meat can be tough, it's important to slice them paper thin across the grain. Look for the lines running along the roast and cut perpendicular to them.

For Fancier Cuts of Meat Once or twice a year, perhaps for a holiday celebration, you may want to cook a fancier cut of meat, like center-cut beef tenderloin. This recipe will work just as well for a more tender cut, and you won't need to worry about slicing the beef as thinly. For beef tenderloin, serve the roast cut into ½-inch (1.5 cm) slices.

What to Do with Leftovers?

ROAST BEEF SANDWICHES

Affordable cuts of beef (like the ones ideal for this roast) make for terrific leftovers. They have a pleasant chewiness and no streaks of solid fat running through them. For a fantastic sandwich, spread some horseradish cream on seeded rye bread and top with cold slices of roast beef. Spread mustard on the other slice of bread and add a handful of arugula leaves on top of the roast beef.

Carnitas Tacos

Serves 6

When you're looking to feed a large group affordably, carnitas is the way to go. You'll love this recipe because it cooks all in one pot. You can use only water, but if you happen to have a bottle of beer in the fridge, pour that in to give the pork an extra dose of flavor.

3 pounds (1.4 kg) boneless pork shoulder (sometimes called pork butt)

Fine sea salt

1 (12-ounce/360 ml) bottle light beer (optional)

3 to 4 cups (720 to 960 ml) water

1 yellow onion, chopped

4 garlic cloves, sliced

1 tablespoon fresh oregano leaves, or 1½ teaspoons dried

2 bay leaves

1 to 2 dried chiles, such as ancho, árbol, or New Mexico

Zest of 1 orange, peeled with a vegetable peeler

Vegetable oil, as needed

Corn tortillas

Lime wedges, for serving

Cut the pork into 1-inch (2.5 cm) cubes and place in a large, heavy-bottomed pot. Season the meat with 1½ teaspoons salt. Pour in the beer and add enough of the water to cover the pork. Bring to a boil.

Skim off any white foam that rises to the surface. Once the foaming has subsided, add the onion, garlic, oregano, and bay leaves. Tear the chiles in half, shake out and discard the seeds, remove the stems, and add the torn chiles to the pot. Add the orange zest. Simmer rapidly, uncovered, until the pork is very tender, about 1 hour 30 minutes.

Fish out and discard the bay leaves and orange peel. (The orange peel can sometimes dissolve, so don't worry if you can't find it.) Cook, stirring often, until all the liquid has evaporated and the pork browns in the remaining fat, about 30 minutes. If the pot becomes too dry because there isn't enough fat, add a splash of oil to prevent burning. Taste and season with more salt as needed.

Warm the tortillas either directly over the flame on a gas stovetop or in a skillet over medium heat until soft. Serve the carnitas with the tortillas and lime wedges.

Doubling the Recipe If you double this recipe, do it in two pots so there's plenty of surface area for the liquid to evaporate and the pork to brown.

Stovetop Macaroni and Cheese

Serves 6

You can't go wrong serving a delicious version of a familiar classic, even for the most special dinner party. Save the toasted bread crumbs, herbs, bacon, and other mix-ins for another dish—this super-creamy macaroni and cheese needs nothing more than its silky sauce. The recipe is simple, but pay careful attention to a few key steps: Generously salt the boiling water, drain the noodles when they're still shy of al dente, and use high-quality extra-sharp cheddar that you've grated yourself.

Fine sea salt

1½ pounds (680 g) macaroni pasta

8 tablespoons (1 stick/115 g) unsalted butter

1 tablespoon cornstarch

¼ teaspoon cayenne pepper

½ cup (120 ml) heavy cream

2 large eggs

1 cup (240 ml) whole milk

1 pound (450 g) extra-sharp cheddar, grated

Freshly ground black pepper

Bring a large pot of generously salted water to a boil. Add the macaroni and cook until just shy of al dente. (Ignore the instructions on the package because they are almost always wrong. Instead, taste a noodle after 4 minutes, and again every minute thereafter. The pasta is ready for the next step when it tastes tender around the edges yet still too firm in the center. It should be a little underdone because it'll keep cooking in the cheese sauce.) Drain the pasta and return it to the empty pot. Add the butter and stir occasionally until the butter melts.

Meanwhile, in a large bowl, whisk together the cornstarch, cayenne, and cream until smooth. Whisk in the eggs and milk.

Once the butter has melted, add the milk sauce and the cheddar to the pot. Cook over medium-low heat, stirring often, until the cheese melts and evenly coats the macaroni. Season with salt and pepper. Serve hot.

Reheating Leftovers Reheating homemade macaroni and cheese is notoriously difficult because the sauce tends to break into an oily mess. To avoid this problem, when reheating, add a few tablespoons of milk per serving of leftover macaroni and cheese and stir several times.

Sample Menus and Game Plans for Entertaining

To prepare for having guests at your home, it can be helpful to write out a game plan that includes all the necessary steps, from shopping for groceries to bringing dessert to the table. Next time you host a party, try using one of the following sample menus and corresponding game plans.

SAMPLE MENU 1 (EASY)

Pizza Night

Serves 4

Negroni for a Crowd (page 117)

Pizza (page 43)

Caesar Salad (page 89)

Tiramisù (page 165)

GAME PLAN

1 Week Ahead
- Make a shopping list.
- Shop for all necessary ingredients. You'll need to double the recipe for the pizza, but it isn't necessary to double the sauce part because there will be enough for two pizzas. When buying toppings, consider making one pizza vegetarian (such as mushroom and olive) and the other nonvegetarian (such as pepperoni).

Night Before
- Make the tiramisù.

- Stir together the gin, Campari, and red vermouth for the Negronis. Chill the mixture in an airtight container in the refrigerator overnight.
- Set the table (see page 54).

Day Of
- About 2 hours before guests arrive, take the pizza dough out of the refrigerator and let it warm to room temperature.
- About 1 hour before guests arrive, make the Caesar salad dressing and croutons. Wash and dry the lettuce for the salad.
- Make the pizza sauce, slice the mozzarella, and prepare the toppings.
- When guests arrive, offer them a Negroni. Make cocktails while you catch up with everyone.
- Preheat the oven for the pizza.
- Fill the water glasses and place a couple of bottles or a jug of chilled water on the table.
- When you're almost ready for dinner, assemble the pizzas and put them in the oven to bake at the same time, switching the position of the pans after 7 minutes.
- Meanwhile, toss the Caesar salad with the dressing and croutons. Set the salad in the center of the table.
- When the pizza is done, tell your friends it's time to eat!
- Once everyone is seated, slice the pizzas and bring them to the table.
- Enjoy dinner.
- Clear the plates and wrap up any leftovers.
- Serve the tiramisù for dessert.
- Once everyone has left, wash the dishes. If you like, share another little Negroni to celebrate the successful pizza party you just hosted.

Summer Lunch Outdoors

Serves 6

Sparkling wine and juice

**Radishes, Butter,
and Flaky Salt (page 216)**

**Manchego-Paprika
Gougères (page 120)**

**Whole Side of Salmon
and Herb Sauce (page 131)**

**Green Rice with
Preserved Lemon (page 101)**

**Strawberry-Rose Shortcakes
(page 162)**

GAME PLAN

1 Week Ahead

- Make a shopping list. Aside from the ingredients for recipes in this book, you'll also need to add sparkling wine and juice. Make sure you triple the ingredients in the recipe for the radishes so that you'll have enough to serve 6.
- Shop for all necessary ingredients.
- Make the *gougères*. Once they have cooled completely, freeze them in an airtight container.

Night Before

- Stir together the strawberries for the shortcakes, cover, and refrigerate. Bake the shortcakes. Once the shortcakes have cooled completely, cover tightly and store at room temperature.
- Gather everything you'll need to set the table (see page 54), but keep it all inside until tomorrow.
- Chill the sparkling wine and juice overnight.

Day Of

- About 2 hours before guests arrive, set the table outdoors. Trim the radishes and

arrange them on a platter with the butter and salt. Leave out at room temperature, covered, so the butter can warm up and soften slightly.
- About 1 hour before guests arrive, start cooking the salmon and make the herb sauce. When the salmon is done cooking, remove it from the oven and let it cool to warm room temperature.
- About 45 minutes before guests arrive, start the green rice.
- About 30 minutes before guests arrive, preheat the oven to 350°F (175°C).
- Just before guests arrive, place the frozen *gougères* on a baking sheet and reheat in the oven for 5 minutes. Keep them warm.

- When guests arrive, offer them sparkling wine or juice. Spend time mingling with everyone and eating radishes and *gougères*.
- Fill the water glasses and place a couple of bottles or a jug of chilled water on the table.
- Tell everyone it's time to eat!
- As people start to sit down, bring the salmon, herb sauce, and green rice to the table. Ask if anyone would like more sparkling wine or juice.
- Enjoy lunch outdoors together.
- While you clear the plates and wrap up any leftovers, your partner can whip the cream and assemble the shortcakes.
- Bring the shortcakes out to the table for dessert.
- Once everyone has left, wash the dishes. A late-afternoon movie at home might be just the thing to enjoy together.

Brunch

Serves 6

Coffee and tea (see pages 204 to 207)

Bloody Marys (page 194)

Fresh fruit

Bacon

**Roasted Bell Pepper
Frittata (page 195)**

**Overnight Cinnamon-Pecan
Buns (page 183)**

GAME PLAN

1 Week Ahead

- Make a shopping list. Aside from the ingredients for recipes, you'll also need to add an assortment of fresh fruit (a mix of your favorite kinds), 18 to 24 slices of bacon, and anything you'll need to make coffee and tea for your guests.
- Shop for all necessary ingredients.

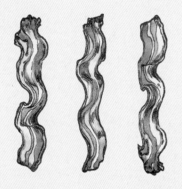

2 Days Before
- Make the tomato juice for the Bloody Marys.

Evening Before
- Set the table (see page 54).
- Make the cinnamon-pecan buns, following the recipe up to the point where you cover the buns in the muffin tin and place them in the refrigerator to chill overnight.

Morning Of

- When you wake up, remove the muffin tin from the refrigerator and let the buns warm at room temperature until puffy, at least 1 hour and up to 3 hours.
- Cut the fruit and arrange it beautifully on a large platter. Set it on the table.
- About 90 minutes before guests arrive, start the frittata. When it's done baking, remove it from the oven and let cool at room temperature.
- Once the frittata comes out of the oven, increase the oven temperature to 400°F (200°C). Line two rimmed baking sheets with aluminum foil and arrange the bacon on the sheets, making sure the bacon slices don't overlap, or they'll stick together. Roast for 30 to 40 minutes, depending on how crisp you like your bacon, rotating the baking sheets after about 20 minutes to promote even cooking. Reduce the oven temperature to 350°F (175°C).
- About 15 minutes before guests arrive, put the buns in the oven to bake while you greet your guests and kick off the brunch. Make sure to set a timer to go off when the buns are done.
- Just before your guests arrive, prepare the garnishes for the Bloody Marys and stir together the tomato juice and vodka in a pitcher. Taste a small glass and, if it is not as strong as you'd like, stir in another splash of vodka.
- When guests arrive, offer them coffee or tea and a Bloody Mary. Sip on the beverages and snack on the fruit.
- Fill the water glasses and place a couple of bottles or a jug of chilled water on the table.
- Tell everyone it's time for brunch!
- As people start to sit down, bring the bacon and frittata to the table. Ask if anyone would like another Bloody Mary.
- Enjoy a leisurely brunch.
- While you clear the plates and wrap up any leftovers, your partner can make more coffee or tea for anyone whose mug is empty.
- Bring the buns out to the table for a final sweet bite.
- Once everyone has left, wash the dishes. You just hosted a lovely brunch—way to go!

Make-Your-Own Taco Feast

Serves 6

**Palomas (page 115)
and beers**

**Chips and Simple
Guacamole (page 217)**

Carnitas Tacos (page 138)

**Ancho Black
Beans (page 98)**

Quick Slaw (page 96)

**Pickled carrots and
red onions (see page 266)**

Lime Crema (page 271)

Hot Sauce (page 267)

**One-Bowl Brownies (page 149)
and cinnamon ice cream**

GAME PLAN

1 Week Ahead
- Make a shopping list. Aside from the ingredients for recipes, you'll also need to add beer, tortilla chips, and cinnamon ice cream. (If you can't find cinnamon ice cream, vanilla would be a fine substitute.)
- Shop for all necessary ingredients. When you buy the avocados for the guacamole, keep in mind that you want them to be perfectly ripe for the day of your dinner party. If they become soft a few days too early, transfer them to the refrigerator, where they will chill without ripening much further.
- Make the pickled carrots and red onions.
- Make the lime crema.
- Make the hot sauce, using New Mexico chiles, if possible.

3 Days Before
- Make the ancho black beans.

1 Day Before
- Make the brownies, adding 2 teaspoons ground cinnamon to the batter.
- Set the table (see page 54).
- Chill the beers overnight.

Day Of
- Cut limes into wedges, place in a little bowl, and store, covered, in the refrigerator.
- At least 3 hours before guests arrive, start the carnitas. It'll cook on the stovetop without needing much assistance from you, so you'll have time to clean up around the house and call your mom to say hi. (When the carnitas are done cooking, keep them warm in their pot over low heat.)
- About 1 hour before guests arrive, make the quick slaw.
- About 40 minutes before guests arrive, slowly warm up the beans in their cooking liquid over very low heat.
- About 30 minutes before guests arrive, make the guacamole. Spoon it into a serving bowl and set it out on the table with a giant bowl of tortilla chips.
- About 10 minutes before guests arrive, sit down together and share a beer. Relax.
- When guests arrive, offer them Palomas or cold beer. Make cocktails and hang out with everyone, eating chips and guacamole.
- When you're nearly ready to sit down for dinner, set the hot sauce, lime crema, pickled carrots and red onions, cabbage slaw, and lime wedges on the table. Fill the water glasses and place a couple of bottles or a jug of chilled water on the table.
- Meanwhile, your partner can warm the corn tortillas either individually over a gas flame on the stovetop or a few at a time in a skillet over medium-low heat. Stack them, wrap in a clean kitchen towel or aluminum foil, and place on the table.
- Tell everyone it's time to eat!
- As people start to sit down, bring out the warmed beans and hot carnitas. Ask if anyone needs another beer.
- Enjoy every bite of dinner.
- Clear the plates and wrap up any leftovers.
- Serve the brownies and ice cream.
- Once everyone has left, wash the dishes. Celebrate and feel proud—you did it!

It's important to celebrate as a couple as much as possible, from the once-a-year holidays to the small triumphs of daily life. Cheer each other on and mark each occasion with something special, maybe even something sweet. On Valentine's Day, skip the dinner reservations, stay in, and enjoy a long, unhurried meal at home, then bake brownies. Did you meet a goal at the office? Warm chocolate chip cookies are exactly what you need. Here's a fun challenge for your wedding anniversary: Re-create the dessert you ate on that special day. A festive layered cake can be perfect for a birthday, but don't forget that you can stick candles in caramel apple pie just as easily. A little something sweet on a special day—or even on an otherwise ordinary day—can become a lasting, meaningful tradition for the two of you.

One-Bowl Brownies

149

Chocolate Chip Cookies

150

Lemon Meringue Kisses

153

Blackberry Crumble

155

Poppy Seed Loaf

157

Birthday Cake

159

Strawberry-Rose Shortcakes

162

Tiramisù

165

Apricot Galette

169

Caramel Apple Pie

171

Classic Vanilla Ice Cream

173

Tangerine Granita and
Barely Whipped Cream

174

One-Bowl Brownies

Makes nine 2½-inch (6.5 cm) square brownies

These brownies come together so easily in one bowl that you won't need much convincing to make them often. Usually flaky sea salt dissolves in batter, but when the batter is very chocolaty, as it is here, the tiny flakes never have a chance to break down completely. You're left with an almost imperceptible crunch of salt, just enough to heighten the chocolate flavors but not so much that it distracts.

12 tablespoons (1½ sticks/170 g) unsalted butter

6 ounces (170 g) unsweetened chocolate, chopped into small pieces

2 cups (400 g) sugar

2 teaspoons pure vanilla extract

3 large eggs

1 cup (125 g) all-purpose flour

½ teaspoon flaky sea salt

Preheat the oven to 350°F (175°C). Line an 8-inch (20 cm) square baking dish with parchment paper, allowing the paper to overhang the sides a bit so that you can easily lift out the brownies.

Bring about 1 inch (2.5 cm) of water to a simmer in a small sauce pot. Set a large heatproof bowl over the pot (make sure the bottom of the bowl doesn't touch the water). Place the butter and chocolate in the bowl and heat gently, stirring occasionally, until melted and well combined. Remove the bowl from the heat, taking care not to splash any water into the chocolate.

Add the sugar, vanilla, and eggs and whisk vigorously for several minutes until very smooth. Stir in the flour and salt. Using a rubber spatula, scrape the batter into the prepared pan and spread it evenly.

Bake until puffed and just barely set, 40 to 50 minutes, depending on how done you like your brownies. They will look slightly domed in the pan (and may have cracked across the top surface) and will feel set, not liquidy, when tapped lightly with your finger. A toothpick inserted into the center won't come out clean; the brownies will still be gooey immediately after baking but will set a little further as they cool to room temperature. Let them cool in the pan, then remove them from the pan using the parchment paper, cut into squares, and serve.

Store leftover brownies, tightly wrapped, at room temperature for up to 3 days.

Chocolate Chip Cookies

Makes 24 cookies

Using a kitchen scale to measure ingredients is the norm in many parts of the world, but it can seem a bit intimidating to someone who is accustomed to working with cups and tablespoons. Give it a try just once, and you'll see firsthand that a scale actually speeds up the process of measuring all the ingredients. It can also cut down on the number of bowls you'll need to wash in the end. Keep a few pointers in mind: Place the scale on a flat surface for accuracy. Locate the tare button (sometimes labeled "zero"). This is the button you'll press to zero out the scale after you add each ingredient. Don't beat yourself up if there are a few grams too many of a main ingredient like flour or sugar. It won't matter much in the end. Last, don't toss out your measuring teaspoons and tablespoons just yet! They, too, have a place. For ingredients you'd add in small quantities (like baking soda, vanilla extract, and salt), a teaspoon remains the simplest and best tool for the job. Try making these chocolate chip cookies using a kitchen scale, but if you find you prefer using cups, don't worry; there will be warm cookies to eat either way! *Pictured with Lemon Meringue Kisses (page 153).*

1 cup (125 g) all-purpose flour

1 cup (115 g) whole wheat flour

¾ teaspoon baking powder

¾ teaspoon baking soda

¾ teaspoon fine sea salt

10 tablespoons (1¼ sticks/140 g) unsalted butter, at cool room temperature

¾ cup packed (160 g) brown sugar

½ cup (100 g) granulated sugar

1 large egg

1½ teaspoons pure vanilla extract

5 ounces (140 g) bittersweet or semisweet chocolate (between 54% and 72% cacao)

Place a small bowl on a kitchen scale and turn on the scale. Measure the all-purpose flour and whole wheat flour, adding them to the bowl. Stir in the baking powder, baking soda, and salt, then set the bowl aside. Place the bowl of a stand mixer (or a large bowl) on the scale and zero the scale. Add the butter, brown sugar, and granulated sugar, zeroing the scale after each addition.

Using a stand mixer fitted with the paddle attachment (or a handheld mixer), beat the butter and sugars together on medium-high speed for 5 minutes, until light and fluffy, using a rubber spatula to scrape down the sides of the bowl after about 2 minutes. Beat in the egg and vanilla. Add the flour mixture and beat on low speed just until you can't see any white streaks of flour. ⟶

Using a serrated knife, chop the chocolate into chip-size pieces. Stir into the cookie dough. Cover the bowl with plastic wrap and refrigerate for at least 1 hour and up to 3 days.

When you're ready to bake the cookies, preheat the oven to 350°F (175°C). Line two baking sheets with parchment paper.

Using two spoons, scoop the dough into 24 balls. Place on the prepared baking sheets, spacing them at least 2 inches (5 cm) apart from one another. Bake until golden brown but still quite soft, 15 to 18 minutes, rotating the baking sheets after 8 minutes or so. Let cool slightly on the baking sheets. The cookies will firm up as they cool. Serve warm.

How to Make Ahead You don't need to bake all the cookie dough at one time. Instead, after scooping the dough balls, place them in a single layer on a baking sheet and freeze until solid, about 3 hours. Transfer the frozen dough balls to a zip-top plastic freezer bag, label with the date, and freeze for up to 4 months. When a craving for chocolate chip cookies hits, place a couple of cookie dough balls on a parchment paper–lined baking sheet and put them straight into a preheated 350°F (175°C) oven. Bake until golden brown but still quite soft, 15 to 18 minutes, rotating the baking sheet after 8 minutes or so.

Buy Excellent Chocolate The quality of the chocolate matters; be sure to choose a premium bar (see Resources, page 294).

Variation

ICE CREAM SANDWICHES

These cookies have just the right amount of structure and chewiness for ice cream sandwiches. Spread 2 big scoops of softened Classic Vanilla Ice Cream (page 173) across the bottom of a cookie, top with another cookie (bottom sides facing in), and chill in the freezer until the ice cream is firm. You can wrap the individual sandwiches tightly with plastic wrap and store in the freezer for up to 3 months, although they'll taste best the first few days after they were made.

Lemon Meringue Kisses

Makes twenty 1½-inch (4 cm) meringues

These airy treats look like puffy little clouds. They are delicious on their own but even better when served with fresh fruit. Plan for plenty of time to cook and cool the meringues. *Pictured with Chocolate Chip Cookies on page 151.*

¾ cup (150 g) sugar

1 lemon

3 large egg whites

Pinch of fine sea salt

¼ teaspoon pure vanilla extract

Preheat the oven to 200°F (95°C). Line a baking sheet with parchment paper.

Place the sugar in a medium bowl. Use a rasp-style grater to zest the lemon directly over the bowl of sugar, letting the finely grated zest fall into the sugar. Using your fingertips, pinch and rub the zest into the sugar until the sugar is pale yellow and fragrant. Squeeze 1 teaspoon of juice from the lemon and mix it into the sugar.

In a large bowl using a handheld mixer or in the bowl of a stand mixer fitted with the whisk attachment (see note), beat the egg whites and salt on medium speed until the mixture holds soft peaks, about 3 minutes. Increase the speed to high and gradually add the lemon-sugar, a little at a time. Beat until the meringue is glossy, voluminous, and stiff, about 5 minutes. Test the mixture by rubbing a tiny bit between two fingers; if it feels gritty, the sugar hasn't completely dissolved and you need to continue beating until it is silky smooth. Stir in the vanilla.

Spoon the meringue onto the prepared baking sheet in 1½-inch (4 cm) blobs with lots of beautiful swoops and peaks, leaving only an inch (2.5 cm) or so between them, as they won't spread much in the oven.

Bake until dry to the touch and hollow-sounding when tapped on the bottom, 3 to 4 hours. Turn off the oven, prop the door open with the handle of a wooden spoon, and let the meringue kisses cool and finish drying for at least 2 hours or up to overnight. Once cool, store in an airtight container at room temperature for up to 1 week.

Use a Clean Bowl and Whisk The most important tip to keep in mind when making these meringues (and this is true for *all* meringues) is that you must use a scrupulously clean bowl and whisk—any grease will interfere with your goal of achieving a light, pillowy texture.

Blackberry Crumble

Serves 6

Make this quick, simple dessert with fresh berries during the summer and try it with frozen berries during the winter. Both versions turn out beautifully. You can use blueberries or raspberries in place of the blackberries, or even a combination, and if the berries are particularly ripe, you might only need to add two tablespoons of granulated sugar to sweeten them. After tossing them with the sugar, taste one to decide if it's sweet enough. *Pictured with Classic Vanilla Ice Cream (page 173).*

8 tablespoons (1 stick/115 g) unsalted butter, cut into small pieces, plus more for the baking dish

1 cup (125 g) all-purpose flour, plus more for the baking dish

2½ cups (12 ounces/340 g) fresh or frozen blackberries

1 teaspoon finely grated lemon zest

1 tablespoon fresh lemon juice

¼ cup (50 g) granulated sugar (see headnote)

½ cup packed (105 g) brown sugar

⅓ cup (30 g) rolled oats

¼ teaspoon ground cinnamon

½ teaspoon fine sea salt

2 teaspoons pure vanilla extract

Classic Vanilla Ice Cream (page 173, or store-bought)

Preheat the oven to 375°F (190°C). Butter and flour a 9-inch (23 cm) square (or equivalent) baking dish.

Combine the blackberries, lemon zest, lemon juice, and granulated sugar in the prepared baking dish. Toss gently with your hands.

In a medium bowl, stir together the flour, brown sugar, oats, cinnamon, and salt. Using your fingertips, rub the butter into the flour mixture until there are no butter pieces larger than a pea. Add the vanilla and squeeze the mixture several times to form clumps. Scatter the streusel topping evenly over the berries. Bake until the topping is golden brown and the berries are bubbling, about 30 minutes.

Serve warm, with a generous scoop of vanilla ice cream.

Crumble vs. Crisp If you prefer to leave out the oats, call it a crisp instead of a crumble. That's the difference between the two desserts—did you know?

Poppy Seed Loaf

Serves 8

There will come a time when you will need a cake, and you will need it fast. Maybe your in-laws or friends have invited you over for dinner at the last minute and asked you to bring a dessert. Or maybe it's Sunday afternoon and you're craving a slice of something sweet and homemade. For those moments when you don't have enough time or energy to run to the grocery store for missing ingredients, turn to this simple loaf cake. The batter comes together in the time it takes for the oven to heat up, and the recipe itself is quite flexible.

Unsalted butter, for the pan

1½ cups (190 g) all-purpose flour, plus more for the pan

2 tablespoons poppy seeds

2 teaspoons baking powder

¾ teaspoon fine sea salt

1 cup (200 g) sugar

2 lemons

1 cup (250 g) plain whole-milk yogurt

3 large eggs

1 teaspoon pure vanilla extract

½ cup (120 ml) neutral-flavored oil, such as canola or safflower

3 tablespoons honey

Preheat the oven to 350°F (175°C). Generously butter and flour a 4½ by 8½-inch (11 by 21 cm/1.5 L) loaf pan.

In a small bowl, stir together the flour, poppy seeds, baking powder, and salt.

Measure the sugar into a large bowl. Use a rasp-style grater to zest the lemons directly over the bowl of sugar, letting the finely grated zest fall into the sugar. (Reserve the zested lemons.) Using your fingertips, pinch and rub the zest into the sugar until the sugar is pale yellow and fragrant. Add the yogurt, eggs, and vanilla. Whisk vigorously until smooth. Add the flour mixture and whisk just until there are no visible streaks of flour. Use a rubber spatula to fold in the oil. When the oil is fully incorporated, the cake batter will have an even, gorgeous sheen. Scrape the batter into the prepared loaf pan. Hold the spatula vertically and drag it lengthwise through the top inch of batter—this technique creates a seam that allows the cake to expand evenly as it bakes. Bake until golden brown and the center of the loaf springs back when lightly pressed, about 1 hour. ⟶

Meanwhile, squeeze 3 tablespoons of juice from the reserved zested lemons into a small saucepan. Add the honey and heat over low heat. As soon as the mixture bubbles, swirl the pan to dissolve the honey, then remove from the heat.

When the cake is done, let it cool in the pan for 10 minutes, then spoon the warm lemon-honey mixture over the top. (Sometimes I poke a few holes in the cake with a fork or toothpick to help it absorb the syrup, but it isn't necessary to do so.)

Let the loaf cool completely before slicing and serving. Store leftovers, tightly wrapped, at room temperature for up to 3 days.

Substitutions No poppy seeds? No problem. If you don't have lemons, forget about the zest and use orange juice for the last step.

NO-RECIPE DESSERTS

Sometimes the simplest dessert is the best dessert. Perfectly ripe fruit has enough natural sweetness to stand on its own, although you might consider pairing a particular fruit with a complementary partner. Here are a few ideas, plus some other no-recipe desserts.

- Fresh fruit

- Cheddar cheese and apple slices

- Stilton cheese and *membrillo* (quince paste)

- A bar of chocolate, broken into pieces

- Whipped cream and ripe berries

- Dates stuffed with mascarpone

- Affogato (hot espresso poured over a scoop of vanilla ice cream)

- Roquefort cheese and walnuts in the shell to crack

- Honey drizzled over pears

- A small glass of amaro

Birthday Cake

Serves 8

This festive layer cake has a texture like that of a lightweight pound cake, thanks to both plain yogurt and whole eggs in the batter. It doesn't need heavy frosting—whipped cream will do, with some jelly swirled into the cream for extra flavor and gorgeous color. Between the cake layers, arrange a not-too-sweet layer of juicy ripe fruit. Blackberries will lend an inky hue, but blueberries, raspberries, and sliced strawberries all work well, as do thin wedges of peach or apricot. Pitted cherries are also wonderful. Maybe it's best to let the birthday girl or guy decide.

1 cup (2 sticks/225 g) unsalted butter, at cool room temperature, plus more for the pans

3 cups (375 g) all-purpose flour

4 teaspoons baking powder

1 teaspoon fine sea salt

½ cup (125 g) plain whole-milk yogurt

½ cup (120 ml) whole milk

2 cups (400 g) granulated sugar

4 large eggs

2 teaspoons pure vanilla extract

Zest and juice of 1 lemon

2 cups (480 ml) heavy cream

¼ cup (30 g) confectioners' sugar

12 ounces (340 g) seedless jam or jelly

12 ounces (340 g) fresh berries, sliced stone fruit, or pitted cherries (see headnote)

Preheat the oven to 350°F (175°C). Butter the sides of two 9-inch (23 cm) round cake pans and line the bottoms with parchment paper cut to fit. (If you dab a little butter on the bottom of the pans, the parchment will stick to it and won't slide around so much.)

In a medium bowl, stir together the flour, baking powder, and salt.

In a large liquid measuring cup or small bowl, mix together the yogurt and milk.

In the bowl of a stand mixer fitted with the paddle attachment, beat the butter and granulated sugar together on medium-high speed until light and fluffy, about 4 minutes. Scrape down the sides of the bowl with a rubber spatula. With the mixer running, add the eggs one at a time, beating until each is incorporated before adding the next. Add the vanilla, lemon zest, and lemon juice and mix well. Add half the flour mixture and half the yogurt mixture to the bowl and mix on low speed until incorporated. Add the remaining flour and yogurt mixtures and mix just until there are no visible streaks of flour. ⟶

Divide the batter between the prepared pans, spreading it evenly and smoothing the tops with a rubber spatula. Bake until the tops of the cakes are golden brown and bounce back when lightly pressed and a toothpick inserted into the center comes out clean, 30 to 35 minutes.

Let the cakes cool in their pans for 5 minutes, then invert the pans on a wire rack, lift the pans off the cakes, peel away the parchment paper, set the cake layers right-side up, and let them cool completely.

In a large bowl, whisk together the cream and confectioners' sugar until airy yet stiff. You want to whip past the point of soft peaks because you'll be frosting the cake with the cream, but be careful not to whip too long, or you'll end up with butter. Stop whipping when you lift the whisk out of the bowl and the cream holds a stiff, pointed peak. Spoon about half the jam or jelly into the bowl of whipped cream and whisk to combine. Depending on the consistency of the jam, there will either be streaks of color cutting through the white cream or tiny flecks of jam throughout, like natural sprinkles.

Place one cake layer on a cake stand or serving plate. Spread the remaining jam or jelly on top of the cake. Arrange the fresh fruit in a single layer over the jam. Top with the second cake layer. Frost the top and sides of the cake with the whipped cream mixture, smoothing it evenly.

Serve immediately. Store any leftover cake, covered, in the refrigerator for up to 2 days. It'll be a little soggier the second day, but it's still tasty.

Strawberry-Rose Shortcakes

Serves 6

Strawberries and roses are botanically related, and their flavors combine beautifully in this easy make-ahead dessert.

1 pound (450 g) fresh strawberries, hulled and halved or quartered

¼ cup (50 g) plus 2 tablespoons sugar, plus more as needed

2 teaspoons fresh lemon juice

1 or 2 drops rose water (see Resources, page 294)

1½ cups (190 g) all-purpose flour, plus more for dusting

½ cup (70 g) cornmeal

2 teaspoons baking powder

½ teaspoon baking soda

¼ teaspoon fine sea salt

4 tablespoons (½ stick/55 g) unsalted butter, cut into small pieces and chilled

1 cup (240 ml) buttermilk or heavy cream, plus more for brushing

1 cup (240 ml) heavy cream

In a medium bowl, combine the strawberries, ¼ cup (50 g) of the sugar, the lemon juice, and rose water. (Be careful not to add too much rose water—it's powerful stuff.) Gently crush the berries with a fork until they release some of their juices. Taste for sweetness and add more sugar, if desired. Set aside to macerate at room temperature for at least 15 minutes or cover and refrigerate for up to 1 day.

Preheat the oven to 425°F (220°C). Line a baking sheet with parchment paper.

In a large bowl, stir together the flour, cornmeal, baking powder, baking soda, salt, and remaining 2 tablespoons sugar. Using your fingertips, rub the butter into the flour mixture until there are no butter pieces larger than the size of a pea. Pour in the buttermilk and stir with a fork until the mixture comes together into a sticky dough.

Turn the dough out onto a flour-dusted surface. Gently pat it into a disc about 2 inches (5 cm) thick. Cut into 6 equal wedges. Quickly shape each wedge into a roundish shortcake. Place them on the prepared baking sheet. Brush the tops with buttermilk and sprinkle with sugar. Bake until light golden brown, about 20 minutes.

Just before serving, beat the cream until it holds soft peaks.

Slice each shortcake in half. Mound about ½ cup (80 g) strawberries on top of the bottom half. Dollop some whipped cream on the strawberries and top with the other shortcake half. Serve.

Tiramisù

Serves 6

In Italian, *tiramisù* means "pick me up." It has an ethereal texture, like how you imagine clouds would feel. Keep this texture in mind when making the tiramisù—beat the egg yolks and sugar until sufficiently airy, use a soft touch to fold in the creamy mascarpone, and gently grip the delicate ladyfinger cookies while dipping them in the espresso.

3 large egg yolks

¼ cup (50 g) sugar

1 cup (8 ounces/225 g) mascarpone cheese

½ cup (120 ml) heavy cream

3 tablespoons rum, or 2 teaspoons pure vanilla extract (see note)

1 to 2 cups (240 to 480 ml) brewed espresso (see page 205) or very strong coffee, cooled to room temperature

1 (7-ounce/200 g) package ladyfingers or Savoiardi cookies

Dark chocolate, for grating

In a large bowl using a handheld mixer, whip the egg yolks and sugar until pale yellow, thick, and satiny, about 4 minutes. Gradually mix in the mascarpone.

In a separate bowl, beat the cream until it holds stiff peaks. Fold it into the mascarpone mixture, then gently stir in the rum.

Pour the espresso into a shallow bowl. (You may need anywhere from 1 to 2 cups, so you can start with just 1 cup and add more if needed.) Dip one ladyfinger into the espresso, turn to soak the other side, then lift it out, allowing the excess espresso to drip back into the bowl. Place the dipped cookie in the bottom of a 1½-quart (1.5 L) serving dish. Repeat to form a single layer of dipped cookies, using half the ladyfingers. Gently spread half the mascarpone mixture over the cookies. Dip the remaining ladyfingers, arranging them in a layer over the mascarpone mixture, then top with the remaining mascarpone mixture. Using a rasp-style grater, grate a shower of chocolate over the top. Cover and refrigerate the tiramisù for at least several hours or up to overnight before serving.

Buy Fresh Eggs This recipe includes raw egg yolks, so be sure to buy fresh eggs from someone you trust, or choose pasteurized eggs.

Rum or Vanilla? Add only as much rum as you like. If you prefer to leave it out entirely, substitute 2 teaspoons pure vanilla extract.

Apricot Galette

Serves 6

A galette is easier to make than a pie. Its filling can be as unfussy as fresh fruit, and if that fruit is bursting with ripeness, you don't even need to bother sweetening it. Make a flaky, crisp-bottomed galette any time of year and fill it with seasonal fruit: a mound of blueberries, the first blushing strawberries, or thinly sliced apples. For a gorgeous late-springtime dessert, use apricot wedges and arrange them facing upward in concentric circles like the petals of a rose.

1 large egg

Cold water

1½ cups (190 g) all-purpose flour

½ cup (60 g) whole wheat flour

¼ cup (50 g) sugar, plus more for sprinkling

¾ teaspoon fine sea salt

1 cup (2 sticks/225 g) unsalted butter, sliced and chilled

9 ripe apricots (about 1¾ pounds/ 800 g total) or drained canned apricots in juice (from one 15-ounce/425 g can)

¼ cup (60 ml) honey, warmed

Whipped cream or plain yogurt, for serving

Crack the egg into a liquid measuring cup and beat with a fork to combine. Add enough cold water to make ½ cup (120 ml) total.

In a large bowl, stir together the all-purpose flour, whole wheat flour, sugar, and salt. Using your fingertips, rub the butter into the flour mixture until the butter pieces are the size of corn kernels. Pour in the egg-water and quickly but gently knead into a ball of dough. Wrap it in plastic, making sure to include any crumbs of flour from the bottom of the bowl, and refrigerate for at least 1 hour and up to 3 days.

Preheat the oven to 375°F (190°C). Line a rimmed baking sheet with parchment paper.

Roll out the dough into a large oval about ⅛ inch (3 mm) thick. Place the dough on the prepared baking sheet and refrigerate for 10 minutes.

Slice the apricots into thin wedges and arrange them on top of the chilled dough, overlapping slightly so that there are no gaps except for a bare 1-inch (2.5 cm) border around the edges. Fold the dough edges over the fruit, then sprinkle the dough and fruit generously with sugar. Bake until the crust is dark golden brown and the apricots are juicy and burnt just at their tips, about 1 hour. Brush the honey over the fruit. Serve each piece of galette with a spoonful of whipped cream or yogurt.

Caramel Apple Pie

Serves 8

People swoon over pie. It could be because we know making pie is a labor of love. Or it might have something to do with how a pie looks—that flaky, golden-brown crust hiding the promise of sticky sweet fruit inside.

Crust

2½ cups (310 g) all-purpose flour, plus more for dusting

2 tablespoons granulated sugar

1½ teaspoons fine sea salt

1 cup (2 sticks/225 g) unsalted butter, sliced and chilled

6 tablespoons (90 ml) ice water, plus more if needed

Caramel

½ cup (120 ml) heavy cream

1 cup (200 g) granulated sugar

¼ cup (60 ml) cold water

2 tablespoons unsalted butter

1 teaspoon pure vanilla extract

½ teaspoon flaky sea salt

Pie Filling and Topping

2 lemons

4 pounds (1.8 kg) tart, crisp apples, such as Granny Smith

½ cup packed (105 g) brown sugar

¼ cup (30 g) cornstarch

1 teaspoon ground cinnamon

½ teaspoon freshly grated nutmeg

1 egg

1 tablespoon heavy cream

Turbinado or other coarse sugar or granulated sugar

Make the crust: In a large bowl, stir together the flour, sugar, and salt. Using your fingertips, rub the butter into the flour mixture until there are no butter pieces larger than the size of a pea. Pour in the ice water and mix just until the dough comes together in a shaggy ball. If it doesn't, add 1 teaspoon ice water and mix again; repeat until the dough comes together. Turn the dough out onto a work surface, divide it into 2 even pieces, and shape each piece into a disc. Wrap the discs tightly with plastic and refrigerate for at least 1 hour and up to 3 days.

Meanwhile, make the caramel: Warm the cream in a small saucepan over low heat. In another small saucepan, combine the granulated sugar and cold water. Cook over medium heat, without stirring, until light golden brown, then swirl the pan gently and cook until the sugar is a deep amber, 12 to 14 minutes total. Gradually whisk the warmed cream into the caramelized sugar and cook until smooth, 1 to 2 minutes more. Remove from the heat and whisk in the butter, vanilla, and salt until well combined and smooth. Let cool. ⟶

Make the filling and topping: Juice the lemons into a large bowl. Peel, core, and thinly slice the apples, adding them to the bowl and tossing to coat the slices in the lemon juice as you go. Mix in the brown sugar, cornstarch, cinnamon, and nutmeg.

On a lightly floured surface, roll out one chilled disc of dough to a 12-inch (30 cm) round. Gently transfer it to a 9-inch (23 cm) pie dish by rolling the dough onto the rolling pin and then unfurling it into the dish. Fold the overhanging dough under itself to create a double-thick edge. Roll out the second disc of dough to a 12-inch (30 cm) round. Cut it into 1-inch-wide (2.5 cm) strips and set the strips aside.

At this point, the caramel should be cool enough to handle and stretchy like chewy toffee. Using two spoons, scoop up mounds of caramel and add them to the bowl with the apple slices. Mix well to evenly distribute. Pour the apple filling into the pie dish, gently packing it down and mounding it in the center. Arrange the strips of dough over the filling in a lattice pattern: Place the longest strip across the middle of the pie and arrange a few more strips on either side of and parallel to the first strip, leaving a little gap between each one. Flip up every other strip, folding them back on themselves, then lay a long strip perpendicularly across the middle of the pie. Unfold the strips and repeat, folding down every other alternate strip and weaving in the other strips, until you've covered the entire top of the pie.

Press the edges of the lattice strips into the bottom crust, trim them flush with the outer crust edge, and crimp using your fingers or a fork. (If using a fork, dip the tines in flour first to prevent them from sticking to the dough.) Beat the egg and cream together, then brush it all over the top crust. Sprinkle generously with turbinado sugar. Chill the fully assembled pie in the freezer for 20 minutes. (This will help the crust keep its shape while it bakes.)

Preheat the oven to 400°F (200°C).

Set the chilled pie dish on a rimmed baking sheet to catch any drips. Bake the pie for 20 minutes, then reduce the oven temperature to 350°F (175°C) and bake until caramelized juices lazily bubble up through the gaps in the lattice top and the top is dark golden brown, about 1 hour more. Don't be shy about baking the pie long enough—it's important to sufficiently heat the filling to activate the cornstarch. Cover the edges with aluminum foil if they are browning too quickly. Let the pie cool for at least 2 hours before serving—the hot, bubbling fruit juices need time to set to the proper consistency of runny jam.

Store the pie, covered, at room temperature for up to 2 days.

Classic Vanilla Ice Cream

Makes about 1 quart (1 L)

A small amount of whiskey adds subtle notes of spice to this vanilla ice cream and also helps with the texture: Since the alcohol doesn't freeze, the finished ice cream is creamy and soft. You can omit the whiskey, if you prefer. Make sure to leave plenty of time for the custard to chill before you churn it. *Pictured with Blackberry Crumble on page 154.*

2 cups (480 ml) heavy cream

1 cup (240 ml) whole milk

⅔ cup (135 g) sugar

Pinch of fine sea salt

½ vanilla bean

6 large egg yolks

1 tablespoon whiskey (optional)

Optional toppings: sprinkles, chocolate sauce, caramel sauce

In a heavy-bottomed medium saucepan, combine the cream, milk, sugar, and salt. Halve the vanilla bean lengthwise and use the dull edge of your knife to scrape all the tiny black seeds into the pot. Drop the scraped bean pod into the pot as well. Warm the mixture over medium heat, whisking occasionally, until the sugar dissolves and the mixture is steaming hot but not yet boiling.

In a medium bowl, whisk the egg yolks to break them up. While whisking, slowly stream in about ¼ cup (60 ml) of the hot cream mixture and whisk until incorporated. Pour the tempered egg yolk mixture into the pot with the hot cream and cook over low heat, stirring continuously with a wooden spoon or rubber spatula, until the cream thickens enough to coat the back of the spoon and registers 170°F (77°C) on an instant-read thermometer, about 5 minutes.

Strain the custard through a fine-mesh sieve into a large bowl. Stir in the whiskey (if using). Cover with a piece of plastic wrap pressed directly against the surface of the custard to prevent a skin from forming and refrigerate for at least 4 hours and up to 3 days.

Pour the chilled custard into an ice cream maker and churn according to the manufacturer's instructions.

Serve right away, with your favorite toppings, or pack the ice cream into a freezer-safe container, place a piece of parchment paper directly on the surface of the ice cream (to ward off ice crystals), cover tightly with the lid, and store in the back of the freezer (where it's coldest) until ready to serve. The ice cream will keep in the freezer for up to 3 months, although it tastes best the first few days after it is made.

Tangerine Granita and Barely Whipped Cream

Serves 4 to 6

You don't need an ice cream machine to make this simple, refreshing granita; all you need are a freezer and a fork. Feel free to substitute your favorite citrus juice for the tangerine juice. Blood orange, grapefruit, and Valencia orange all work well, but they may require a little more or less sugar, depending on the particular fruit. Tasting the juice is the surest way to find out. Plan ahead and leave at least four hours for the granita to freeze.

1 cup (240 ml) fresh tangerine juice

Juice of 1 Meyer lemon or regular lemon

2 tablespoons granulated sugar, plus more as needed

1 tablespoon orange liqueur or gin (optional)

½ cup (120 ml) heavy cream

1 teaspoon confectioners' sugar

½ teaspoon pure vanilla extract

In a small pot, combine the tangerine juice, lemon juice, and granulated sugar. Heat over medium-low heat, stirring occasionally, until the sugar completely dissolves. Taste a small spoonful. If it isn't sweet enough, add another tablespoon of sugar, stir to dissolve, then taste again. Repeat as needed. Remove from the heat and stir in the orange liqueur (if using). Pour the mixture into an 8-inch (20 cm) square or equivalent size dish, cover tightly, then freeze for at least 4 hours. At least once every hour, use a fork to lightly scrape the surface to break up the frozen juice into tiny crystals. (If you forget to scrape the granita and it freezes solid, don't worry—it will still work. Just let it thaw very slightly, then use a fork to scrape and break it up into tiny crystals.) Once the granita has been scraped to a fluffy consistency, cover the dish and freeze until ready to serve.

A few minutes before serving the granita, combine the cream, confectioners' sugar, and vanilla in a medium bowl. Whisk by hand until the cream holds very soft peaks. It's better to underwhip than overwhip here. As soon as the cream thickens and holds floppy peaks, stop whisking.

Layer a spoonful of granita in the bottom of a pretty glass or small bowl. Top with a dollop of barely whipped cream, followed by another spoonful of granita and more whipped cream. Serve promptly.

Cooking Outdoors

Food tastes better outdoors. Whenever you can, find a way to enjoy your meals together under an open sky. It can be as easy as sitting in your own backyard or packing a picnic and going to the park. For cooking outdoors, either a gas or charcoal grill will do. And every so often, get away from it all and go camping. Here are a few tips and recipe suggestions.

GRILLING

If you're using a gas grill, it needs only to be turned on and preheated. If you're working with a charcoal grill, you'll need to first start the charcoal. To do so, gather the necessary tools: a chimney starter, some newspaper, enough charcoal to fill the chimney starter, and matches. Crumple individual sheets of newspaper and pack them into the bottom of the starter, then fill it with charcoal. Strike a match and touch the flame to the crumpled newspaper. It will catch fire and begin to heat up the charcoal. The charcoal is ready when it's glowing red hot, with white speckles. This usually takes 15 to 20 minutes. Carefully dump the hot charcoal into the bottom of the grill, spreading it out evenly. Let the grill grate heat up sufficiently, and you're good to go!

HOW TO BUILD AND COOK OVER A WOOD FIRE

This is an important survival skill—and a fun way to cook dinner. If you were a Boy or Girl Scout, you may already know that the first step is choosing the right spot for a fire. Ideally, a fire should be built in a designated fire ring with an iron grate for cooking, but if this isn't an option, choose a flat clearing at least 12 feet (4 m) away from your tent. You'll need to gather dry logs, kindling (thin pieces of wood) or twigs, a stack of newspaper, and matches. Crumple individual sheets of the newspaper and pile them up in a small mound in the center of the fire ring. Arrange the kindling or twigs over the paper in an overlapping crosshatch pattern. If it's cold or windy, use more kindling than you think you'll need to start the fire. Stack two logs on top of the kindling. Strike a match and touch the flame to the newspaper in several places. The kindling will catch first, then the logs. If neither happens, crumple more paper, shove it underneath the wood, and blow gently until you see flames. Give the iron grate plenty of time to heat up. The flames will burn off any gunk left on the grate by the previous cook. Roaring flames can be romantic, but the best fire for cooking is actually just tiny flames from red-hot embers. When flames touch food, they impart a sooty flavor. You want smokiness but not sootiness, so make sure to wait until the burning logs break apart into embers. Place the food you're cooking on the part of the grate closest to you and reserve the back of the fire area as a hot zone where you'll add logs as needed. When you're done, remember to extinguish your fire completely before you leave. Hot ashes can be doused with water or snuffed with dirt.

RECIPES FOR EXTRAORDINARY CAMP FOOD

MAIN COURSES

Cast-Iron-Skillet Steak with Blue Cheese Butter (page 40)

Diner-Style Burgers (page 35)—serve with salt-and-pepper potato chips instead of fries

Hearty Tabbouleh with Chickpeas and Feta (page 69)—drain and rinse the chickpeas at home

SIDES

Simple Leafy Salad and Mustard Vinaigrette (page 84)—wash and dry the lettuce at home

Sicilian Fennel-Citrus Salad (page 93)

Quick Slaw (page 96)

DRINKS

Negroni for a Crowd (page 117)—pour into a large jug at home, and bring lots of ice

Beer and wine (see pages 111 and 110)

SWEETS

One-Bowl Brownies (page 149)—bake at home and bring with you; they'll keep well, tightly wrapped, at room temperature for up to 3 days

No-Recipe Desserts (see page 158)

Don't forget about s'mores!

BREAKFASTS

Challah French Toast (page 199)—skip the compote and serve with maple syrup instead

California-Style NYC Breakfast Sandwiches (page 181)

Bloody Marys (page 194)—prepare the tomato juice at home

SNACKS

Radishes, Butter, and Flaky Salt (page 216)

Sardines, Baguette, and Lemon (page 223)

Simple Guacamole (page 217)

Chocolate Toast (page 229)

Pan con Tomate (page 211)—set a cast-iron skillet directly on the grate over the fire ring

Prosciutto and Ripe Fruit (page 212)

Breakfast Anytime

On a Saturday morning, when you have a little time to spend with each other, cooking breakfast or brunch together is a terrific way to reconnect and make plans for the coming days. And when it's your sweetheart's birthday, what a treat it is to make a special breakfast for her or him. But the truth is, you can cook breakfast together anytime. Breakfast sandwiches taste delightful at lunchtime, an omelet served alongside a green salad is a light, elegant dinner, and I've never met a person who doesn't perk up at the prospect of waffles or crêpes late at night. On a cold winter day, breakfast for dinner makes for a very cozy evening. In this chapter, you'll find recipes to turn to on hectic weekday mornings, leisurely weekends, and every hour in between.

California-Style NYC Breakfast Sandwiches

Serves 2

New York City may be known for its bagels, but among the locals, the BEC (shorthand for bacon, egg, and cheese, served on a soft roll) reigns supreme. If you stand on a busy sidewalk in Manhattan during the morning commute hours and look around, you'll see people devouring these fuss-free breakfast sandwiches on their way to work. BECs are designed for speed, like much of New York. They come double-wrapped in waxed paper and aluminum foil, and they're just the right size to eat out of hand. They are also endlessly adaptable. As glorious as a classic BEC is, I can't help but add a few California flavors: sliced avocado, a handful of arugula, and a squeeze of lemon juice. *Pictured with a Chia Berry Parfait for a Busy Morning (page 182).*

3 or 4 slices bacon or pancetta

1 tablespoon unsalted butter, plus more for the rolls

2 large eggs

Fine sea salt and freshly ground black pepper

2 small soft rolls, cut in half

2 slices any kind of cheese (optional)

1 small or ½ large avocado, thinly sliced

2 handfuls of arugula

½ lemon

Flaky sea salt

Cook the bacon in a skillet over medium heat until crisp and browned.

Meanwhile, in small skillet, melt the butter over medium-low heat. Whisk the eggs just until the yolks and whites are combined, add them to the pan, and cook, stirring often with a fork, until scrambled and set. Season with fine salt and pepper. (Alternatively, you could fry the eggs sunny-side up in the rendered bacon fat.)

Toast the rolls in a toaster, under the broiler, or in a skillet over medium heat and butter them generously. If using the cheese, immediately place a slice on each hot roll so that it melts. (If the cheese doesn't melt, warm the cheese toast under the broiler, watching it carefully to make sure it doesn't burn.) Top with the cooked egg and bacon. Layer on the avocado and arugula. Squeeze a little lemon juice over the arugula and season with a pinch of flaky salt. Top with the other half of each roll.

Double, Please When you're really hungry, make it two eggs per sandwich.

Chia Berry Parfaits for a Busy Morning

Serves 2

It's often the case that only after showering, getting dressed, packing a lunch, and running out the front door do you realize you've forgotten about breakfast. This recipe will come in handy because it requires nothing of you during those busy early hours—all the cooking (which is truly more like assembling) happens the night before. As you're leaving home, reach into the fridge and grab one of these portable parfaits. It can be enjoyed wherever you're going or en route. *Pictured with California-Style NYC Breakfast Sandwiches on page 180.*

1⅓ cups (330 g) plain whole-milk yogurt

⅔ cup (70 g) rolled oats

1 tablespoon chia seeds

½ cup (70 g) frozen berries, such as raspberries, blackberries, or blueberries, or a combination

2 tablespoons honey

In a bowl, stir together the yogurt, oats, and chia seeds. Spoon half of this mixture into the bottoms of two 8-ounce (240 ml) glass jars. Top evenly with the berries and honey. Spoon the remaining yogurt mixture into the jars. Cover and refrigerate overnight, until the oats have softened and the berries have thawed and created a thin sauce between the yogurt layers.

The parfaits can be stored in the refrigerator for up to 3 days.

Overnight Cinnamon-Pecan Buns

Makes 12 buns

The more you can do ahead of time to prepare for guests, the better. This is especially true when those guests are coming over in the morning for breakfast. On the night before their arrival, set the table (see page 54) and gather all the serving platters and utensils you'll need. Empty your dish rack or dishwasher. While the two of you are making sure everything is in order, you can let the dough for these buns rise. Just before bed, put the rolled buns in the refrigerator. Take them out first thing in the morning, and once they've come to room temperature, into the oven they go! By the time your guests arrive, your kitchen will be filled with the enticing smells of cinnamon, toasted pecans, and sugar.

Dough

1 cup (240 ml) whole or 2% milk

1 (¼-ounce/7 g) package active dry yeast

3 tablespoons plus 2 teaspoons granulated sugar

1 teaspoon fine sea salt

1 large egg

3 cups (375 g) all-purpose flour, plus more for rolling

8 tablespoons (1 stick/115 g) unsalted butter, melted

Filling

4 tablespoons (½ stick/55 g) unsalted butter, melted and cooled slightly, plus more for the pan

1 cup packed (215 g) brown sugar

1 tablespoon ground cinnamon

1 cup (110 g) chopped pecans

1 teaspoon finely grated orange zest

Make the dough: Using a microwave or in a small saucepan on the stove, warm the milk to body temperature (about 100°F/37°C), then pour it into the bowl of a stand mixer or a large bowl. Stir in the yeast and 2 teaspoons of the sugar. Cover the bowl with a clean kitchen towel and set aside until tiny bubbles form on the surface of the yeast mixture, about 5 minutes. (If the yeast doesn't foam at all, toss it out and start again with new yeast.) Add the remaining 3 tablespoons sugar, the salt, egg, flour, and butter. Using the dough hook of the stand mixer or a wooden spoon, mix until a soft dough forms. Knead on low speed or by hand until satiny and smooth, 5 to 7 minutes. Cover the bowl, place in a warm, draft-free spot, and let rise until doubled in size, about 1 hour. →

Make the filling: Generously butter a 12-well muffin tin. In a medium bowl, stir together the brown sugar, cinnamon, pecans, and orange zest.

On a lightly floured surface, roll the dough out to a 14 by 10-inch (35 by 25 cm) rectangle. Brush about half the melted butter over the dough, then sprinkle the cinnamon-pecan mixture evenly on top, leaving a ½-inch (1.5 cm) border. Drizzle the remaining melted butter over the pecan filling. Starting from one of the long sides, roll the dough tightly into a cylinder, gently lifting and tucking the dough under to keep it tight. Cut the cylinder crosswise into 12 equal pieces. Place one piece in each well of the prepared muffin tin. Cover with plastic wrap and refrigerate overnight.

The next day, remove the muffin tin from the refrigerator and let the buns warm at room temperature until puffy, at least 1 hour and up to 3 hours.

About 15 minutes before you're ready to bake the buns, preheat the oven to 350°F (175°C).

Place the muffin tin on a rimmed baking sheet to catch any drips. Bake until evenly golden brown, 23 to 29 minutes. (The exact time depends on how long the buns have been out of the refrigerator before baking. Check them after 23 minutes and then again every couple of minutes after that, removing them from the oven when they're evenly golden brown.) Invert the muffin tin to remove the buns, place them on a platter, and let cool for a few minutes before serving.

Banana-Blueberry Bran Muffins

Makes 12 muffins

These muffins are moist but not dense, with deep, toasted grain and molasses flavors. They're not exactly the health food kind you might be imagining, though they are packed with wheat bran, an excellent source of fiber, and will keep you feeling full for hours.

8 tablespoons (1 stick/115 g) unsalted butter, melted, plus more for the pan

1 cup (65 g) wheat bran

1 cup (125 g) all-purpose flour

1 teaspoon baking soda

2 teaspoons baking powder

¾ teaspoon fine sea salt

½ cup (80 g) dried blueberries

½ cup packed (105 g) brown sugar, plus more for sprinkling

1 cup (250 g) plain whole-milk yogurt

2 large eggs

2 tablespoons molasses

2 teaspoons pure vanilla extract

1 or 2 large bananas, thinly sliced

Preheat the oven to 375°F (190°C). Line a 12-well muffin tin with paper liners or grease each well with butter (the muffins will puff up while they bake, so make sure to grease the flat part of the tin around the edge of each well even if you're using paper liners).

In a medium bowl, stir together the wheat bran, flour, baking soda, baking powder, salt, and dried blueberries.

In a large bowl, whisk together the brown sugar, yogurt, eggs, molasses, vanilla, and melted butter. Add the bran mixture to the yogurt mixture and stir until just combined.

Spoon the batter into the prepared muffin tin, dividing it evenly among the wells. Arrange 2 or 3 banana slices on top of each muffin, overlapping them slightly like shingles on a house. Sprinkle the banana slices with brown sugar. Bake until the edges are darker and the centers of the muffins feel set and springy when tapped with a finger, 25 to 30 minutes. (It's difficult to judge the muffins' doneness by color alone because they are already brown to begin with. Look for the tops to lose their wet sheen—when they appear matte, they're done.) Let cool in the tin for a few minutes, then transfer to a wire rack and let cool completely.

Whole Wheat Crêpes

Makes eight or nine 8-inch (20 cm) crêpes

Lacy-edged crêpes make for such a festive breakfast. You can serve them with yogurt, fresh berries, or your favorite jam (see toppings suggestions on the next page). The crêpe batter needs an overnight rest in the refrigerator, so plan ahead. But know that the batter will keep for a few days, which means crêpes for breakfast on a weekday morning isn't a completely farfetched idea.

⅔ cup (75 g) whole wheat flour

⅓ cup (40 g) buckwheat flour

2 tablespoons sugar

¼ teaspoon fine sea salt

2 large eggs

1 teaspoon pure vanilla extract

2 tablespoons unsalted butter, melted, plus more butter for the pan

¾ cup (180 ml) milk, plus more if needed

¼ cup (60 ml) dark beer

In a medium bowl, combine the whole wheat flour, buckwheat flour, sugar, and salt. Whisk in the eggs, vanilla, melted butter, milk, and beer. Cover and refrigerate overnight.

The next morning, you'll notice that the batter has thickened. It should be just a touch thicker than heavy cream. If it's too thick, whisk in a little more milk.

Heat an 8-inch (20 cm) pan (preferably a French steel pan) over medium heat. Swirl in a little butter. While tilting and rotating the pan, pour in a ladleful of batter. Move the pan until the batter evenly covers the bottom. Cook just until the edges darken and look dry, 30 seconds to 1 minute. Use a heatproof spatula to lift up an edge, grasp it gently with your fingertips, and swiftly flip the crêpe over. Cook on the second side for about 10 seconds, until it browns in a few places. Transfer the crêpe to a plate. Repeat to cook more crêpes, stacking them on the plate. Add butter to the pan as needed; you shouldn't need much, maybe a small piece every 2 or 3 crêpes.

You can serve the crêpes hot out of the pan, or keep them warm in a 200°F (95°C) oven until you're done cooking. They can also be covered and stored in the refrigerator for a few days, and reheated in a pan. ⟶

Beer in the Batter A splash of dark beer makes the crêpes wonderfully tender and light and also adds a subtle malty flavor.

Crêpe Toppings

LEMON AND SUGAR

Squeeze a generous amount of lemon juice over a cooked crêpe and sprinkle with a spoonful of granulated sugar.

ORANGE AND HONEY

Squeeze a generous amount of orange juice over a cooked crêpe and drizzle with some honey.

JAM AND FRUIT

Spread an even layer of jam across a crêpe, then fold the crêpe in half and then in half again. Place the folded crêpe on a platter and repeat with the remaining crêpes, overlapping them slightly on the platter. Scatter a handful of fresh berries over the crêpes and dust their tops with confectioners' sugar.

YOGURT AND MAPLE

Spoon some plain whole-milk yogurt across a crêpe, then fold the crêpe in half and then in half again. Drizzle with real maple syrup.

Sambal-Spiced Breakfast Sausages

Serves 4 to 6

Making sausages at home is a stress-free and creative endeavor, especially when you shape little patties in the palm of your hand and don't have to worry about stuffing the meat into casings. This recipe takes its flavor cues from Southeast Asia and includes ginger, lime juice, and fiery fresh chiles, key ingredients in the Indonesian hot sauce called sambal. Add as much chile as you like.

1 pound (450 g) ground pork

2 garlic cloves, minced

1 (1-inch/2.5 cm) piece fresh ginger, peeled and finely grated or minced

1 teaspoon rice vinegar

1½ teaspoons fish sauce

1 tablespoon fresh lime juice

1 to 3 fresh hot chiles, such as bird's-eye, habanero, or cayenne, seeded and minced

1 teaspoon fine sea salt

1 tablespoon canola oil

In a large bowl, combine the pork, garlic, ginger, vinegar, fish sauce, lime juice, chile(s), and salt. Using your hands, mix well. Shape into 12 patties, each about 2 inches (5 cm) across.

Heat a large skillet over medium heat. Add the oil and heat for 1 minute, then add half the patties. Cook until browned on the first side, 2 to 4 minutes. (You can use a splatter screen to shield your stovetop.) Flip and cook until browned on the second side and cooked through, 2 to 4 minutes more. Transfer to a plate. Repeat to cook the remaining patties. (You won't need to add more oil for the second batch; just give the pan a swirl to distribute the rendered fat.)

What to Do with Leftovers?

RICE BOWLS

Cook some brown rice (see page 101) and season it with a splash of rice vinegar. Warm up the sausages and serve them over the rice, with whole fresh basil leaves. If you like, add a soft-boiled egg and some kimchi (page 238, or store-bought).

Made-to-Order Omelet

Serves 1

Cooking a single serving of any dish for someone feels like such a loving gesture. And an omelet, which is best hot out of the pan and still tender in the middle, is a wonderful dish to master for those times when you or someone you love hungers for a quick, comforting meal. Economical and as welcome for breakfast as it is for lunch or a light dinner, an omelet can be filled with any kind of soft cheese (see page 230 for ideas) or a spoonful of leftovers. Sautéed greens, a few flakes of roasted salmon (see page 131), or some braised chicken (see page 125) would work excellently. You could even try a spoonful of thinly sliced kimchi (see page 238) or a couple of chopped spiced olives (see page 213).

1 tablespoon fresh tender herbs, such as chervil, basil, chives, or flat-leaf parsley

2 large eggs

Fine sea salt and freshly ground black pepper

1 tablespoon unsalted butter

Fillings, as desired (see headnote)

Heat a 6-inch (15 cm) nonstick or seasoned carbon-steel pan over medium-low heat for about 3 minutes.

Meanwhile, finely chop the herbs and place them in a medium bowl. Crack in the eggs. Add 2 pinches of salt and a few grinds of pepper, and stir with a fork until the whites and yolks are combined. (For a tender omelet, don't overbeat the eggs. Stop whisking when there are still a few streaks of white visible.)

Melt the butter in the preheated pan and tilt the pan to evenly coat with the butter. Pour in the eggs and immediately use the rounded back of the fork to stir the eggs around in the pan, dragging the cooked egg at the edges toward the center. After a few seconds of stirring, lift and tilt the pan so that any uncooked egg flows into the exposed parts of the pan. Spoon any desired fillings into the middle of the omelet, then cook for a few seconds, undisturbed, until the bottom is set. Use a heatproof rubber spatula to fold the omelet over itself in half or into thirds. Cook for a few more seconds, then flip the omelet onto a plate and serve.

Add a Salad Do like the French and place some lightly dressed lettuce on the plate after finishing the omelet. (Try the Simple Leafy Salad and Mustard Vinaigrette, page 84.) The runny bits of egg that didn't quite make it onto the fork will coat the leaves, making the salad a little richer.

Bloody Marys

Serves 4 to 6

The secret to an extraordinary Bloody Mary is homemade tomato juice. To make it, all you have to do is quickly blend fresh tomatoes with a handful of seasonings. Yes, making your own tomato juice will take a little longer than opening a can, but once you taste how much brighter the flavors are, you'll never go back. *Pictured with Roasted Bell Pepper Frittata on page 196.*

1½ pounds (680 g) ripe red tomatoes (about 4 medium), quartered

¼ to ½ small jalapeño, seeded

1 tablespoon fresh lime juice, plus 1 lime, sliced thinly into wheels

2 teaspoons sherry vinegar

½ teaspoon fine sea salt, plus more if needed

Ice cubes

4 to 6 celery stalks with leaves attached

1½ cups (12 ounces/360 ml) vodka or tequila, plus more as needed

Freshly ground black pepper

In a blender, combine the tomatoes, jalapeño, lime juice, vinegar, and salt and blend until very smooth. Taste for seasoning, adding another pinch of salt if needed and a little more jalapeño if you want. (The tomato juice can be made ahead and refrigerated, covered, for up to 3 days. Stir well before using.)

Just before you're ready to serve the cocktails, fill 4 to 6 glasses with ice cubes and garnish each with 1 lime wheel and 1 celery stalk (see note for more garnish options).

In a pitcher filled with ice cubes, combine the vodka and fresh tomato juice. Stir with a long spoon until chilled, about 1 minute. Taste a spoonful. If it's not as strong as you'd like, stir in another splash of vodka. Pour into the prepared glasses, garnish each with lots of black pepper, and serve right away.

Garnishes Galore Bloody Marys are made to be customized. You can garnish them with all kinds of delicious additions: olives, cucumber slices, cooked shrimp, grated fresh horseradish, and more.

Celery Salt Rim Make your own celery salt by toasting 1 tablespoon celery seeds in a small, dry pan for 1 minute, then mixing in 1 tablespoon flaky sea salt. Before filling the serving glasses with ice cubes, spread the celery salt out on a small plate. Cut 1 lime into wedges and use it to wet the rim of each glass. Dip the rim into the salt.

Roasted Bell Pepper Frittata

Serves 6

A frittata is a wonderful dish to share among friends because it looks impressive, is familiar without being boring, and tastes great warm, at room temperature, or even chilled. *Pictured with Bloody Marys on the following pages.*

2 large red bell peppers

2 tablespoons sherry vinegar

1 tablespoon capers, rinsed

Leaves from 4 sprigs fresh thyme

Leaves from 4 sprigs fresh oregano

1 cup (20 g) fresh flat-leaf parsley leaves, chopped

Fine sea salt

4 tablespoons (60 ml) olive oil

½ cup (120 g) crème fraîche (store-bought, or see page 271 and leave out the lime)

12 large eggs

½ cup (55 g) grated semi-firm cheese, such as Fontina or white cheddar (optional)

1 small yellow onion, chopped

Roast the bell peppers directly over a gas flame on the stovetop or under a broiler until completely charred, turning the peppers often to evenly char all sides. Transfer them to a paper bag (or place in a bowl and tightly cover with plastic wrap) and let steam for a few minutes.

Preheat the oven to 300°F (150°C).

When the peppers are cool enough to handle, peel off and discard the charred skin. Discard the stems and seeds. Resist the temptation to rinse the peppers—it's much better to have a few seeds stubbornly clinging to the pepper than to wash away all those flavorful juices. Tear each pepper into ½-inch-wide (1.5 cm) strips and place in a large bowl. Mix in the vinegar, capers, thyme, oregano, parsley, 2 teaspoons salt, and 2 tablespoons of the olive oil. Add the crème fraîche, eggs, and cheese (if using) and beat with a fork just until combined.

In a 12-inch (30 cm) oven-safe skillet, heat the remaining 2 tablespoons oil over medium-high heat. Add the onion and ½ teaspoon salt and cook, stirring, until softened, about 5 minutes. Pour in the egg mixture. Use a wooden spoon to stir for 90 seconds. Transfer the skillet to the oven and cook until just barely set in the center, about 20 minutes. To test for doneness, poke the tip of a knife into the center of the frittata; if the egg runs and seems thin and liquidy, cook for another few minutes before testing again. Be careful not to overcook the frittata, or it won't have that wonderful custard-like texture. The frittata can be served warm or chilled, but it doesn't reheat so well because it overcooks.

Challah French Toast with Grapefruit-Cranberry Compote

Serves 4

Making compote is a lot like making jam, but it's quicker and much less precise. You can make it while the coffee brews. After preparing the citrus segments for this grapefruit-cranberry compote, you'll be left with extra grapefruit and orange juice—just the right amount to sip on while you gather the ingredients for the French toast.

Compote

¼ cup (60 ml) water

¼ cup packed (55 g) brown sugar

1 cinnamon stick

2 whole cloves

¼ cup (30 g) dried cranberries

1 large grapefruit

2 blood oranges

French Toast

4 large eggs

1 cup (240 ml) half-and-half

2 teaspoons pure vanilla extract

¼ cup packed (55 g) brown sugar

1½ teaspoons ground cinnamon

Pinch of freshly grated nutmeg

¼ teaspoon fine sea salt

1 loaf challah, cut into 8 slices, each about 1 inch (2.5 cm) thick

3 tablespoons unsalted butter

Confectioners' sugar, for dusting

Make the compote: In a small pot, combine the water, brown sugar, cinnamon stick, and cloves and bring to a boil, stirring until the sugar dissolves. Cook for 1 minute, then add the dried cranberries, boil for 2 minutes, and turn off the heat. Remove and discard the cinnamon stick and cloves. (Don't worry—it's not the end of the world if you can't find the cloves.)

Cut the grapefruit in half along its equator. Use the tip of a small, sharp knife to cut out each little segment of fruit, slicing on either side of the white pith and around the outer edge. Place the grapefruit segments in a fine-mesh strainer set over a bowl to catch any juices. Once you've cut out all the segments, squeeze each grapefruit half over the segments to collect the juice. Repeat with the blood oranges. (If the oranges are the size of baseballs or smaller, it will be easier to cut them according to the technique on page 93.) ⟶

Transfer the citrus segments to the pot. Add 2 tablespoons of the strained citrus juice and enjoy the rest in a glass with a few ice cubes. Gently stir the compote. (The compote can be stored, covered, in the refrigerator for several days.)

Make the French toast: Crack the eggs into a pie dish. Add the half-and-half, vanilla, brown sugar, cinnamon, nutmeg, and salt. Use a fork to stir well.

Heat a large pan over medium heat for a couple of minutes.

It's best to cook the French toast in batches so as not to crowd the pan. Start by soaking 2 of the challah slices in the egg mixture, flipping to coat both sides and to fully saturate the challah. Slide a little less than 1 tablespoon of butter into the hot pan and, once it melts, lift the slices out of the egg mixture and place them in the pan. Cook for 1 minute or so on the first side, then peek underneath one slice to see how brown it is. Once it is nicely browned, flip and cook on the second side for another minute or two, until both sides are crisp on the outside but still soft on the inside. Stack the 2 slices of French toast on a warm plate. Repeat to cook the remaining challah slices.

Dust each stack of French toast with confectioners' sugar, spoon some compote on top, and serve right away.

Doubling the Recipe If you're doubling this recipe to serve more people, set a heatsafe plate in a 200°F (95°C) oven and move each piece of cooked French toast to the plate to keep warm while you cook the other slices.

Leftover Compote? The compote is a wonderful accompaniment to other dishes, too—try it stirred into a simple bowl of oatmeal.

Yeasted Waffles

Serves 4 to 6

I first came across the idea of adding yeast to waffle batter in Marion Cunningham's *The Breakfast Book*. I've added whole-grain flour and included a few details in the instructions about how to proof the yeast, melt the butter, and warm the milk as swiftly and efficiently as possible. You'll have to make the batter the night before you cook the waffles, and anything you do right before going to bed should be easy. The batter rises overnight while you sleep. You can choose to leave it out at room temperature, which leads to an extra-yeasty, sourdough-like flavor, or you can refrigerate it if the thought of leaving a milk-based batter out for hours in a warm kitchen makes you nervous. You could also try making the dairy-free variation described on the next page.

½ cup (120 ml) warm water

1 (¼-ounce/7 g) package active dry yeast

2 tablespoons sugar

8 tablespoons (1 stick/115 g) unsalted butter, plus more for the waffle iron

2 cups (480 ml) milk

½ teaspoon fine sea salt

1 cup (125 g) all-purpose flour

1 cup (115 g) whole-grain flour, such as whole wheat, rye, or spelt

2 large eggs

½ teaspoon baking soda

Maple syrup, for serving

Pour the water into a large bowl. Sprinkle the yeast and sugar evenly over the top and stir to dissolve. Cover the bowl with a clean kitchen towel and set aside until tiny bubbles form on the surface of the yeast mixture, about 5 minutes. (If the yeast doesn't foam at all, toss it out and start again with new yeast.)

Meanwhile, melt the butter in a small saucepan over medium heat. You can cook it until it browns, if you like the nutty flavor of browned butter, or simply until it has melted. Remove the pan from the heat and pour in the milk. Mixed together, the hot butter and cold milk should be about the right lukewarm temperature for the yeast. If the mixture feels warmer than your body temperature, let cool slightly before adding it to the foamy yeast. Whisk in the salt and both flours. Cover with plastic wrap and let rise at room temperature for at least 6 hours or, ideally, overnight; or refrigerate for at least 6 hours and up to 3 days.

Just before you're ready to cook the waffles, preheat a waffle iron. Preheat the oven to 200°F (95°C).

Whisk the eggs and baking soda into the batter. ⟶

Butter the inside surfaces of the iron (even nonstick waffle irons require this step). Spoon ¼ to ½ cup (60 to 120 ml) of the batter onto the waffle iron, close the lid, and cook until crisp and golden brown, following the manufacturer's instructions. Transfer the cooked waffle to a heatsafe plate or serving platter and keep warm in the oven while you cook the remaining batter.

Serve the warm waffles with maple syrup. Freeze any uneaten waffles in a zip-top plastic freezer bag and reheat them in a toaster.

Variation

DAIRY-FREE YEASTED WAFFLES

Substitute neutral-flavored oil (such as grapeseed or canola) for the butter and use sweetened almond milk in place of the dairy milk. It's not necessary to heat the oil for the batter, although you could warm the almond milk to just under body temperature for the yeast.

Coffee and Tea

Going to a café for a cup of coffee or tea can be a lovely way to find a moment of respite in the middle of a crazy day. But you can also just as easily make your own coffee and tea at home—and you'll save a good amount of money if you do.

COFFEE

There's such a comfort to the ritual of making and drinking coffee. Here's everything you need to know about how to store coffee beans and which style of grinder to use, plus recipes and tips for perfecting pour-over, stovetop espresso, and cold brew.

STORING COFFEE BEANS

Buy whole beans and look for a recent roasting date on the package. When possible, avoid beans that were roasted more than two weeks earlier. If the beans came in one of those pouches with a one-way valve that lets air out but not in, keep them in there. If you bought them in bulk or they came in a waxed brown paper bag, transfer the beans to an airtight container when you get home and store them at room temperature out of direct sunlight—not in the refrigerator or freezer, where the porous beans would quickly absorb unwanted smells. Save your most recently roasted coffee beans for hot preparations like pour-overs and espresso and use your less-than-fresh beans for cold brew.

GRINDER

For the most nuanced and vibrant coffee, grind the beans mere seconds before brewing. Grinders (sometimes called coffee mills) come in a few different styles: manual burr grinders (lightweight and portable, excellent for camping and picnics), electric blade grinders (with sharp blades that slice the beans into irregular bits), and electric burr grinders (with powerful teeth that evenly crush the beans).

Professional baristas exclusively use electric burr grinders, which are precise, reliable, and quick. They aren't cheap and can sometimes cost even more than coffeemakers, but electric burr grinders are worthy investments.

POUR-OVER

Elegant in its simplicity, pour-over coffee requires no fancy gadgets—all you need is a filter and a cone-shaped dripper that sits atop your mug. If you think you might regularly brew more than a single serving, consider the timeless Chemex, which comes in larger sizes and is so iconic that it is part of the permanent design collection at the Museum of Modern Art. Here's the step-by-step process for a perfect pour-over for one.

1 Bring 2 cups (480 ml) water to a boil in a teakettle or saucepan.
2 Fold the filter, if necessary, and place it in the cone-shaped dripper, then rinse it with hot water to remove its papery taste. (This initial step also warms up the dripper and mug below.) Let the water drip through completely and rest in the mug for a moment, then discard it. Place your pour-over setup on a kitchen scale, zero the scale, and keep a stopwatch handy.
3 Grind coffee beans to a medium-fine texture, like that of kosher salt or coarse sugar. Measure 3 tablespoons (21 g) ground coffee into the filter. Zero the scale.
4 Start the timer and pour in enough hot (about 207°F/97°C) water to saturate the grounds. Stir gently to break up any clumps.
5 After about 40 seconds, pour in more hot water, evenly submerging the grounds, until the water level almost reaches the top of the dripper. The scale should indicate you've added about 380 grams of water total.
6 After 2 minutes, your mug will be full of hot, freshly brewed coffee. Don't worry if there's water left in the filter—just discard it and enjoy your coffee.

STOVETOP ESPRESSO

The classic Italian moka pot reliably brews delicious coffee on the stovetop. Here's how to use one.

1 Pour cold water into the lower chamber of the pot, filling it no higher than the little belly-button valve on the side.
2 Grind coffee beans to a texture like that of fine sea salt. Fill the funnel-shaped basket of the moka pot with ground coffee, but do not pack it down. Brush away any loose grounds on the rim.
3 Tightly screw the top onto the base.
4 Place the pot on the stovetop over medium heat and open the lid. If you're using a gas stove, adjust the heat so that the flames do not come up the sides of the pot.
5 As soon as coffee flows into the top chamber, close the lid and reduce the heat to low. Brew until the top chamber is full and the gurgling sound changes to a steam hiss.
6 Serve immediately in tiny espresso cups. You may prefer to dilute the coffee with hot water (for an Americano) or pour the coffee (full-strength or diluted) over ice and add a splash of cream.

COLD BREW

There are various tools and specially designed pots for making cold brew coffee at home. At a minimum, you need only a large glass jar plus some cheesecloth or a thin, clean kitchen towel for straining the brew. Make sure to plan ahead, as this method takes the longest from the moment you begin the process until your first sip, although the brewing method is largely hands-off, and the cold brew coffee keeps well for up to 1 week.

1 Grind 2 ounces (55 g) coffee beans to a texture like that of coarse cornmeal.
2 In a 1-quart (1 L) glass jar, combine the ground coffee and 2 cups (480 ml) water. Stir gently.
3 Cover the jar and set aside at room temperature or in the refrigerator to steep for 12 hours.
4 Strain the cold brew through a cheesecloth-lined fine-mesh sieve or a thin kitchen towel into a clean jar.
5 To serve, dilute the cold brew with as much cold water, milk, or cream as you like and enjoy over ice. Cold brew coffee keeps well in an airtight container in the refrigerator for up to 1 week.

TEA

Whether you're brewing a strong black tea to wake you up in the morning or a calming, caffeine-free tea to enjoy just before bed, the following tips and guidelines will help you brew well every time.

TEA VARIETIES

All true tea leaves come from *Camellia sinensis*, a bushy plant native to East Asia. The leaves are harvested and then processed in various ways depending on the type of tea being made. There are five primary tea types: white, green, oolong, black, and Pu-erh. White and green tea leaves are dried, rolled, and packed but never given an opportunity to oxidize. Oolong tea undergoes partial oxidation, while black tea is fully oxidized and Pu-erh is aged. You can see the results of these distinct processing methods in the final color of the teas. Their flavors are also quite different. White tea is subtle and mild, green tea is bright and vibrant, oolong often has complex layers of flavor, black tea is bold, and Pu-erh tastes fermented and funky in a good way.

BUYING AND STORING TEA LEAVES

In an ideal world, you'd be allowed to touch the leaves and taste a cup of tea brewed from them before buying. Specialty tea shops will often encourage this, and the process of choosing which tea to take home can be such a delight. Whenever possible, buy loose-leaf tea leaves from a vendor you trust. Unfortunately, there's a certain amount of fraud in the tea industry, especially among sellers of rare Pu-erh. All high-quality tea leaves will feel pliable, look relatively consistent in size, and smell pleasant. As soon as you get home, transfer the tea leaves to an airtight container and store at room temperature, away from direct sunlight. Properly stored tea can keep for one to five years, depending on the type of tea. You'll know when your tea has passed its prime because it will smell and taste lifeless. Old tea isn't dangerous; it's just not as delicious as it could be.

HOW TO BREW LOOSE-LEAF TEA

First and foremost, use exceptionally pure water and high-quality tea. Filtered water is best. Heat the water to just under a boil. For oolong, green, and white teas, let the water cool slightly before steeping the leaves. When brewed with too-hot water, these teas can taste bitter. Measure the appropriate amount of tea leaves (this varies by type of tea, but 3 grams per 1 cup/240 ml water is a solid starting point) into the straining basket of a teapot and pour in the hot water. Steeping time also depends on the type of tea: As a general rule of thumb, green tea needs to steep for only 2 to 3 minutes; Pu-erh steeps for 3 to 4 minutes; oolong and black teas benefit from 3 to 6 minutes of steeping, or longer if you plan to add milk to black tea; and white tea steeps for 4 to 6 minutes. Always ask the vendor or check the tea package for more details on steeping. One of the benefits of high-quality tea leaves is that they can be steeped two, three, and sometimes even four times without the resulting tea diminishing too much in flavor. Steeping times are generally longer for each successive steep.

MASALA CHAI

Originating in India, masala chai is a wonderful combination of strong black tea, milk, and warming spices such as ginger, cinnamon, cloves, cardamom, and black pepper. There are numerous regional variations, and it's fun to create your own house version. Here's a solid starting-point recipe that makes enough chai for four people.

1 Bring 3 cups (720 ml) water to a simmer in a small saucepan over medium-high heat.
2 Add ¼ cup (10 g) loose-leaf black tea or 4 black tea bags; 1 (2-inch/5 cm) piece fresh ginger, peeled and sliced; 1 cinnamon stick; 3 whole cloves; 3 black peppercorns; and 4 whole cardamom pods, smashed. Simmer for about 5 minutes.
3 Add 1 cup (240 ml) milk and ¼ cup packed (55 g) brown sugar. Cook, stirring, until the sugar dissolves completely and the chai is hot.
4 Strain into mugs and serve.

TISANE

A tisane is an infusion made by steeping fresh herbs. Technically it can't be called tea because it's not made from the leaves of the *Camellia sinensis* plant, but it has the same soul-soothing qualities and, as a bonus, contains no caffeine, making it the perfect beverage to enjoy late at night. Mint is classic, and lemon verbena is heavenly after a big meal. Try lemon balm, lemongrass, thyme, sage, and even dried flowers like rose and lavender. The preparation couldn't be simpler: Just pour boiling water over the herbs or flowers and steep until they flavor and color the tea to your liking. You can make a tisane in a teapot—the glass ones allow you to see the beautiful color of the fresh herbs while they steep—or you can make tisanes in individual mugs. Tear or lightly crush the fresh leaves before dropping them directly into the teapot or mugs. Don't worry about measuring an exact amount of herbs. A small handful per cup (240 ml) of hot water is usually plenty. Pour in the hot water and let the tisane steep for a few minutes. (If making by the mug, just sip around the floating herbs.)

Snacks

Your kitchen is the heart of your home. It's the place where you come together and catch up about how your days went, preferably while enjoying a little snack. Homemade snacks are so much better than the store-bought versions—and far more romantic, too. They don't take a long time to prepare, and they're welcome at nearly all hours. One sweet thing you can do for the guy or girl you love is to make him or her a favorite snack. How about sharing a bowl of buttery popcorn for a movie night at home? Or maybe some guacamole and chips on a lazy weekend afternoon? And if you're not sure which snack to make for your sweetheart, you can't go wrong with chocolate toast.

Pan con Tomate

Serves 2

Called *pa amb tomàquet* in Catalan, this toast rubbed with tomato transports you to Spain but comes together easily in your own kitchen. For a party, try tripling the recipe and serving the separate components—garlic bread, halved tomatoes, sherry vinegar for drizzling, and salt for sprinkling—all together on a platter, and let your friends join in on the fun of assembling the dish.

Olive oil

2 (1-inch-thick/2.5 cm) slices country-style bread

1 garlic clove, peeled

1 large, ripe tomato

Sherry vinegar

Flaky sea salt

Generously brush olive oil on both sides of the bread slices. Place the bread in a large skillet over medium-high heat and cook until toasted on the first side. Flip and cook on the second side, pressing down with a spatula to promote even browning, until toasted. Remove the bread from the pan and, while it is still hot, rub each slice with garlic—the rough surface of the toast will grate the garlic onto the bread. Slice the tomato in half through its equator and rub one half across each toast. The tomato will fall apart, leaving only the skin behind in your hand. Drizzle a little oil and vinegar over the toasts and sprinkle generously with flaky salt. Serve right away.

Prosciutto and Ripe Fruit

Serves 2 to 4

One reason this classic combination works so well is that it brings together salty and sweet. Buy excellent imported or domestic prosciutto (see Resources, page 294) and choose a selection of ripe fruits. You can cut the fruit into bite-size pieces, which are ideal for arranging on a platter. Alternatively, you can leave the fruit in larger pieces, which are better if you plate each dish individually and prefer to eat it with a fork and knife. *Pictured with Warmed Spiced Olives and Radishes, Butter, and Flaky Salt on page 214.*

4 ounces (115 g) sliced prosciutto

Fresh fruit, such as peaches, nectarines, pears, apricots, cantaloupe, and figs

6 tablespoons (90 ml) olive oil

⅓ cup (50 g) whole almonds

1 small bunch flat-leaf parsley

½ Preserved Lemon (page 246, or store-bought)

Tear each piece of prosciutto into long strips, and let warm to room temperature or for as long as you can stand before you get too hungry.

While the prosciutto warms, prepare the fruit (see headnote for ideas). Arrange it on a large platter or individual plates.

Heat a small skillet over medium heat. Add 1 tablespoon of the oil and the almonds. Cook, stirring often, until the almonds are lightly toasted, about 5 minutes. Transfer the toasted nuts to a cutting board, let them cool slightly, then coarsely chop them and place in a bowl. Finely chop the parsley leaves and add them to the bowl. Scoop out and discard the squishy inner part of the preserved lemon, finely chop the peel, and add it to the bowl. Pour in the remaining 5 tablespoons (75 ml) oil and stir well to combine.

Drape the prosciutto over the fruit and spoon the almond-herb sauce over everything. Serve.

What Else to Serve? Complementary snacks like a bowl of Warmed Spiced Olives (opposite), toast drizzled with olive oil, and crumbled hunks of Parmigiano-Reggiano can seamlessly accompany the prosciutto and fruit on the platter, turning this uncomplicated dish into a bountiful appetizer.

Warmed Spiced Olives

Serves 4 to 6

Olives taste remarkably more nuanced warmed or at room temperature than they do chilled. It takes only a few minutes to warm them in a pan with a scattering of spices, and it is well worth the effort. If you're serving guests, put out a small bowl for the olive pits. Make sure to sample an olive and drop the pit in the bowl so your guests don't feel shy about doing the same. *Pictured with Prosciutto and Ripe Fruit and Radishes, Butter, and Flaky Salt on the following pages.*

2 cups (360 g) olives with pits (a single type or an assortment; see note)

1 teaspoon cumin seeds

½ teaspoon coriander seeds

1 teaspoon fennel seeds

1 dried chile de árbol

3 tablespoons olive oil

1 garlic clove, smashed with the back of a knife and peeled

2 teaspoons sweet paprika

3 strips lemon zest, peeled with a vegetable peeler

Place the olives in a colander and rinse under running water. Set aside to drain.

In a small, dry saucepan, toast the cumin, coriander, fennel, and chile over medium-low heat until fragrant, 1 to 2 minutes. Add the oil, garlic, and paprika. Stir in the olives. Add the lemon zest strips. Reduce the heat to low and cook, stirring often, until the olives are warmed through, about 5 minutes. Serve warm, with an empty small bowl on the side for pits.

Which Type of Olive? Choose your favorite type of olive or opt for an assortment of sizes and colors—for green olives, try the large, buttery Castelvetrano, the gigantic Cerignola, or the oblong and crisp picholine; for purple olives, you can't go wrong with the beloved Kalamata, but don't forget about the tender Gaeta and the anise-flavored Niçoise. If you can, try to add a few wrinkly oil-cured black olives to the mix as well.

Radishes, Butter, and Flaky Salt

Serves 2

Even if you haven't tasted radishes, butter, and salt together, you'll know intuitively what to do with them. You'll also develop your own personal preferences about how much butter you like to scoop up with the radish and how big a pinch of salt to sprinkle on top. Try sampling different radish varieties: French Breakfast, Easter Egg, watermelon, and black radishes are all beautiful and delicious. *Pictured with Prosciutto and Ripe Fruit and Warmed Spiced Olives on the preceding pages.*

1 bunch radishes (any color)

2 tablespoons unsalted butter, at cool room temperature (see note)

Flaky sea salt

Rinse the radishes and trim off any stringy roots (but keep the leafy tops if the greens are perky). Arrange the radishes on a plate. Swipe the butter along one edge of the plate and mound a tiny pile of the salt near the butter. Serve.

Eat the Greens Radish greens are perfectly edible—they taste peppery like watercress. To keep the radishes crisp and their greens lively, store them in a shallow bath of cold water in the refrigerator, and eat them as soon as possible.

Substitutions Lime Crema (page 271) or plain crème fraîche can stand in for the butter. So can a soft and mild-flavored cheese like fresh ricotta or La Tur.

Simple Guacamole

Serves 4 to 6

If the avocados are good, you don't need to add more than lime juice and flaky salt to make fabulous guacamole. No tomato, onion, or any other ingredient is necessary. Ripe avocados will mash easily, but it can be more visually appealing to leave the avocado in bite-size pieces. Tossing the avocado gently with your hands will soften and blur the edges of the pieces just enough, without completely changing their satisfyingly firm texture. Serve with salty tortilla chips, Fried Fish Tacos (page 51), or Carnitas Tacos (page 138). *Pictured with Scorched Shishito Pepper Quesadillas on the following page.*

2 large ripe avocados

1 tablespoon fresh lime juice

¼ teaspoon flaky sea salt,
plus more if needed

Cut the avocados in half, remove the pits and peels, and cut the halves into bite-size pieces. Place them in a bowl and add the lime juice and salt. Using your hands, toss gently to coat the avocado pieces with the lime juice. Taste and add another pinch of salt if needed.

Scorched Shishito Pepper Quesadillas

Serves 2

The shishito is a petite, slender chile grown widely in Japan. Most are mild and sweet, with approximately the same level of heat as a bell pepper, but occasionally one will be fiery enough to surprise you. There's no way of knowing which pepper that will be. You can count on one rogue shishito in every handful or so. This only makes eating shishitos all the more fun! Cook them quickly in a smoking-hot cast-iron skillet. They're delicious just like that, with a shower of flaky salt, but even better tucked into these cheesy quesadillas. Add guacamole and chips to turn this snack into a lunch. *Pictured with Simple Guacamole (page 217).*

1 tablespoon neutral-flavored oil, such as canola or grapeseed, plus more as needed

1¼ cups (6 ounces/170 g) shishito peppers, stemmed

Flaky sea salt

8 corn tortillas

4 ounces (115 g) semi-firm cheese, such as Monterey Jack, sliced or grated

Heat a large cast-iron skillet over medium-high heat for 1 minute.

Add the oil and peppers to the hot skillet, stir to coat the peppers in the oil, and cook, without stirring, for 3 minutes, until the peppers are dark brown in a few places. Cook, stirring only once or twice, until tender, 2 to 3 minutes. Transfer to a plate and sprinkle with salt.

Reduce the heat under the skillet to medium-low. Place 2 tortillas in a single layer in the skillet. Toast on the first side for 1 minute, then transfer to the plate with the peppers. Add another 2 tortillas to the skillet and toast on the first side for 1 minute. Flip. Scatter about half the cheese over the tortillas, dividing it evenly. Place about 8 scorched peppers over the cheese on each tortilla. Top with the toasted tortillas, with the toasted side facing the peppers. Flip and cook until the cheese melts, 1 to 2 minutes. Repeat to cook the remaining quesadillas, adding a little more oil to the pan if it looks dry.

Cut each quesadilla in half, if you like, and serve hot.

Where to Find Shishito Peppers? Shishitos have become so popular here in the United States that even Trader Joe's now sells them. They can often be found in farmers' markets as well.

Tuna Salad Lettuce Wraps

Serves 2 to 4

Tuna salad lettuce wraps make a fine lunch or a quick, simple, and comforting dinner after an exhausting day. You scoop up a spoonful of tuna salad, push it into the middle of a lettuce leaf, and wrap the lettuce around it like a burrito. Make the wraps as small or as large as you like. Try serving the tuna salad with savory seeded crackers as well as lettuce. A cracker topped with tuna salad is like a mini tuna sandwich.

2 (5-ounce/140 g) cans of tuna in oil

¼ cup (55 g) mayonnaise

1 tablespoon Dijon mustard

2 tablespoons olive oil

2 or 3 cucumber pickles, finely chopped

Fine sea salt and freshly ground black pepper

Snipped chives

1 small head butter lettuce, leaves separated, washed and dried

Savory seed-topped crackers (optional)

Rinse the tuna in a fine-mesh sieve, then place in a medium bowl. Add the mayonnaise, mustard, olive oil, and pickles. Mix well. Season with salt and pepper.

Serve, garnished with snipped chives, with the lettuce and crackers (if using) on the side.

Sardines, Baguette, and Lemon

Serves 2

I can take no real credit for this recipe. In fact, I'm not sure it can even be considered a recipe. It's more accurately a timeless combination of ingredients, a trio you'll be glad to know.

1 (3.75-ounce/105 g) can sardines (see note)

1 lemon

1 baguette

Open the can of sardines. Cut the lemon in half.

Tear off a piece of baguette. Use your fingers to push the sardine fillets off their center bones. Drape the fillet over the bread, squeeze a little lemon juice on top, and enjoy.

Which Sardines to Buy? There are tons of great canned sardines to try. Look for nonsmoked sardines packed in olive oil (not water or any other kind of oil). Spain and Portugal are both renowned for their tinned seafood, so keep your eye out for delicious imports from those countries.

Sweet-and-Salty Mixed Nuts

Serves 6

An egg white, whisked until frothy, gives these roasted nuts a satisfying, crunchy coating. It's very difficult to eat only a few nuts. Their saltiness makes them a fine accompaniment to a cocktail, and their sweetness means they are equally at home alongside dessert, possibly with cheese. *Pictured with Stovetop Popcorn (page 226).*

½ cup packed (105 g) brown sugar

2 teaspoons fine sea salt

2 teaspoons ground cinnamon

1 teaspoon ground ginger or ground allspice

Pinch of cayenne pepper

1 large egg white

3 cups (345 g) mixed raw nuts, such as walnuts, almonds, and pecans

Preheat the oven to 325°F (160°C). Line a rimmed baking sheet with parchment paper.

In a small bowl, stir together the brown sugar, salt, cinnamon, ginger, and cayenne.

In a large bowl, whisk the egg white until frothy. Add the nuts and the spice mixture, then stir until the nuts are evenly coated. Spread them out on the prepared baking sheet. Bake, stirring once or twice, until fully roasted, about 30 minutes. To test for doneness, cut a nut in half and check that its center is golden brown. Let cool completely on the baking sheet before serving.

The nuts keep well, stored in an airtight container at room temperature, for up to 3 weeks.

A Sweet Gift These mixed nuts will keep well for weeks. You can pack them into a little glass jar, tie it with a bow, and give them as a gift.

Stovetop Popcorn

Serves 2 to 4

Making popcorn at home is easy, quick, and affordable. Somehow the joyful *ping-ping* sound of kernels popping never gets old. You can customize the popcorn to suit your mood. Drizzle with some butter, if you're feeling classic, or sprinkle on just about any spice in your pantry. I've tried fennel seeds, za'atar, red pepper flakes, and many more. Add the spices directly to the bowl that the popcorn will be served in. If you add them to the pot that the popcorn cooks in, they just end up stuck to the sides and can easily burn. *Pictured with Sweet-and-Salty Mixed Nuts on the preceding page.*

3 tablespoons olive oil

⅓ cup (75 g) popcorn kernels

1 tablespoon unsalted butter

Fine sea salt

In a large, heavy-bottomed pot, heat the oil over medium heat. Add the popcorn kernels and tilt the pot to evenly coat the kernels in the oil. Cover the pot with a lid, leaving it slightly ajar. As soon as you hear the first kernel pop, remove the pot from the heat, shake vigorously (with the lid on!) to move the kernels around, then let the pot cool down for 1 minute. You might hear other kernels popping even though the pot isn't over the heat.

Return the pot to medium heat, leaving the lid slightly ajar again, and cook until there are 30 seconds or so between pops, 3 to 5 minutes. It is much better to have a few unpopped kernels than even one burned kernel, so don't leave the pot on the heat for too long. Transfer the popcorn to a medium serving bowl.

Melt the butter in a small pot, then drizzle it over the popcorn. Sprinkle with a few pinches of salt and toss well. Serve warm.

Variations

MIDDLE EASTERN POPCORN

Instead of butter, warm 1 tablespoon olive oil in a small pot. Stir in 2 teaspoons Middle Eastern Spice Mix (page 275) or store-bought za'atar, 1 teaspoon sesame seeds, ½ teaspoon ground sumac, and ¼ teaspoon fine sea salt. Pour the seasoned oil over the popped popcorn, toss well, and serve.

ITALIAN POPCORN

Instead of butter, warm 1 tablespoon olive oil in a small pot. Stir in 1 teaspoon fennel seeds, ¾ teaspoon red pepper flakes, and ½ teaspoon fine sea salt. Pour the seasoned oil over the popped popcorn, toss well, and serve.

INDIAN POPCORN

Melt the 1 tablespoon unsalted butter or ghee in a small pot. Stir in 1 teaspoon mustard seeds, 1 teaspoon ground turmeric, ½ teaspoon cumin seeds, and ½ teaspoon fine sea salt. Cook the spices in the butter for a few minutes, until fragrant. Pour the seasoned butter over the popped popcorn, toss well, and serve.

Chocolate Toast

Serves 2

This sweet and comforting snack feels like home. It is the kind of food you'd be hard-pressed to find on a restaurant menu. It's something more private, made when you need to quell hunger pangs and, more important, soothe. There's nothing fancy about it—and that is precisely why it is so marvelous. Make it often.

1 bar dark chocolate (at least 70% cacao)

Unsalted butter

2 thick slices country-style bread

Pinch of flaky sea salt (optional)

Use a vegetable peeler to create thin curls of chocolate by running the blade of the peeler along the length of the chocolate bar. You can make as many or as few curls as you like—it all depends on how chocolaty you want your toast.

Heat a large skillet over medium heat. Butter both sides of the bread. Place the bread in the skillet and cook, pressing down with a spatula every so often, until golden brown and toasted on the first side. Flip. Pile the chocolate curls in the center of each slice of bread. Cook until the chocolate shines and is right on the verge of melting—this takes only a moment. Sprinkle with the salt, if desired, and enjoy warm.

Cheese

Buying cheese can be intimidating—cheeses come in many shapes and sizes, and their names are often unfamiliar to an English speaker—but don't worry, there are some simple rules that make it easier to understand cheese. Just give it a shot and you'll have such fun getting to know the quirky and delicious world of cheese makers, sellers, aficionados, and *affineurs* (people who buy cheese directly from producers, age it, and care for it before selling it when the cheese reaches its prime). Find the best cheese shop close to you and befriend the staff. Come with your questions and desires, and be honest about your budget. There's so much to taste and discover.

You can serve cheese as an appetizer, as part of the main course, before or with dessert, or after dessert. Any time is a great time for cheese! When composing a cheese platter, choose cheeses that complement one another, whether because of their flavors, textures, or appearances. Ideally, the cheeses will complement one another in all three areas. To help guide your choices, you might like to pick a theme for the platter. Here are a few ideas.

- All-American
- World Tour
- Mixed Milk (one cheese made from cow's milk, one from sheep's milk, and another from goat's milk, or, conversely, a selection of cheeses made from all three)
- Always Blue
- Young and Aged (a fresh cheese and a mature one)

EXCELLENT ACCOMPANIMENTS

Cheese pairs well with a wide assortment of food and drinks: fruits (fresh or dried), bread or crackers, jam, honey, and more. You might find that a cheese tastes a certain way by itself but then transforms in flavor when eaten in the same bite with a sip of wine. Here are some accompaniments worth trying.

- Baguette
- Toasted nuts
- Thinly sliced raw fennel
- Fresh fruit
- Dried fruit
- Jam and other preserves
- Honey
- Wine
- Beer

CHEESE RULES

To get the most out of the cheeses you buy, follow these three simple rules.

1 Taste cheese before buying whenever possible.
2 Store cheese loosely wrapped in parchment paper (not plastic) in the refrigerator—cheese is a living food and needs to breathe.
3 Always serve cheese at room temperature.

RECIPES FOR COOKING WITH CHEESE

- Grilled Cheese (page 25)
- Chicken Parm (see page 28)
- Green Lasagne (page 72)
- Scorched Shishito Pepper Quesadillas (page 219)
- Kale-Mushroom Strata (page 78)
- Yours and Mine Pizza Night (page 43)
- Leek and Goat Cheese Tart (page 63)
- Food Processor Potato Gratin (page 102)
- Manchego-Paprika Gougères (page 120)
- Ravioli (page 235)
- Stovetop Macaroni and Cheese (page 141)

RICOTTA

CAMEMBERT

PARMIGIANO-REGGIANO

VALENÇAY

CHEDDAR

ROQUEFORT

Kitchen Projects

When you have the chance to spend a few hours in the kitchen together, these recipes will give you something delicious to show for it. Kitchen projects, like other kinds of projects, are satisfying at least in part because of the effort they require and also because you're rewarded with seeing (or in this case, tasting) the results of all your hard work. For some recipes in this chapter, the effort is mostly an exercise in patience. Spiced orange bitters need three weeks to infuse before they're ready. Preserved lemons take even longer. Once made, however, they'll both keep well for years. The more ephemeral foods, like apple cider doughnuts and a loaf of bread, freeze remarkably well. So, the next opportunity you get, spend a day laughing, talking, and working in the kitchen together.

Ravioli

Serves 4 to 6

Making fresh pasta dough is easy. To easily roll out the dough, however, you'll need a pasta machine, but it's not a big problem if you don't have one—a rolling pin works, although slowly (and is actually more traditional). As with many time-honored crafts, the key to homemade pasta is practice. Your first few ravioli will probably look a bit wonky, and that is fine. They'll still taste great, and there's no doubt that whomever you serve them to will be touched by all the care you put into them.

Pasta Dough

3 cups (375 g) all-purpose flour, plus more for rolling

3 large eggs

3 large egg yolks

2 tablespoons olive oil

Filling

1 pound (450 g) fresh spinach or dandelion greens, tough stems trimmed

¾ cup (185 g) whole-milk ricotta

½ cup (55 g) freshly grated Parmigiano-Reggiano cheese

1 large egg yolk

Fine sea salt and freshly ground black pepper

Make the pasta dough: Measure the flour into a large bowl and make a well in the center, like a volcano. Add the eggs, egg yolks, and oil to the well. Use a fork to stir, gently scraping in flour from the sides a little at a time. When the dough becomes too stiff to stir, use your hands to mix it, then turn it out onto a cutting board and knead it into a ball. If it's too crumbly to hold together, work in a few drops of water, just a little at a time, until the dough holds together. Cover with plastic wrap or a clean kitchen towel and let rest at room temperature for 30 minutes.

Meanwhile, prepare the filling: Bring a large pot of salted water to a boil. Add the spinach and cook until just wilted, about 1 minute. Drain in a colander. Rinse under cold water, then squeeze out every last drop of liquid. (You can use a kitchen towel to wring out the greens, but just know that afterward it might be green forever.) Chop the greens extremely fine, then place them in a medium bowl. Mix in the ricotta, Parmigiano, egg yolk, ½ teaspoon salt, and lots of pepper. Refrigerate the filling until ready to use.

Use your hands to flatten the dough ball into a disc, then cut it into 12 equal pieces. Work with one piece at a time and keep the other pieces covered with the clean kitchen towel. Using a pasta machine ⟶

or rolling pin, roll out each piece into a long sheet, at least 2 inches (5 cm) wide and just under 1 millimeter thick (the second-thinnest setting on most machines). If using a machine, start by further flattening each piece with a rolling pin before passing it through the machine rollers. Begin with the rollers opened to their widest setting. After the first pass, fold the dough lengthwise over itself into thirds, as if you were folding a letter, then pass it through on the widest setting again. Repeat once more to further knead the dough, then decrease the width setting of the machine by one notch and crank the dough through the rollers. Continue decreasing the width setting and passing the dough through until the sheet is very thin and long. If it seems like too much dough to handle at one time, you can cut the dough into short pieces, but make sure each piece remains at least 2 inches (5 cm) wide. If the dough sticks to the machine, sprinkle it lightly with flour. Stack the rolled pasta sheets between damp kitchen towels on a baking sheet. If the dough feels moist and it's a humid day, skip the damp towels and instead sprinkle flour generously between the pasta sheets to prevent sticking.

Working with one sheet at a time, dust off any flour and spoon about ½ tablespoon of filling every 3 inches (7.5 cm) or so along the length of the pasta. Place another sheet of pasta on top, lining up the edges evenly. Use your fingertips to press down around each mound of filling, squeezing out any trapped air and pressing the pasta sheets together. If the pasta refuses to stick to itself, dab the parts that need to stick with a little water and press again. Trim the top and bottom edges and cut between the ravioli to separate them. For straight sides, use a small knife; for frilly sides, use a fluted rolling cutter. Cover with a clean kitchen towel and refrigerate if not cooking right away. You might be left with a small amount of filling—refrigerate it, covered, and use it the next day in an omelet (see page 193).

To cook, bring a large pot of generously salted water to a boil. Add the ravioli, stir, and cook until al dente, 4 to 6 minutes. Drain and sauce as desired (see opposite for suggestions).

Plan Ahead for the Sauce As for which sauce to serve with these ravioli, choose any you like: sage brown butter, brodo, simple tomato, or another favorite. The best time to make the sauce is after you've shaped and filled the ravioli. They take only a few minutes to cook, so make sure the sauce is ready to go.

Sauces for Ravioli

SAGE BROWN BUTTER

For every 4 servings of ravioli, melt 6 tablespoons (¾ stick/85 g) unsalted butter in a large pan over medium-high heat. Add 2 pinches of fine sea salt and a small bunch of fresh sage leaves (about 12 medium-size leaves) to the pan. Cook, stirring or swirling occasionally, until the butter browns and the sage crisps. Transfer the cooked ravioli directly to the pan of sauce along with a ladleful of cooking water and toss until coated.

BRODO

For every 4 servings of ravioli, bring 2 cups (480 ml) chicken broth (see page 47) to a simmer. Taste for seasoning, adding salt if needed. Divide the broth evenly among four wide, shallow bowls. Add the cooked ravioli directly to the broth. Drizzle a little olive oil over the top and serve.

SIMPLE TOMATO SAUCE

In a medium sauce pot, bring 1 (28-ounce/795 g) can whole peeled tomatoes and their juices to a simmer. Add 1 large onion, cut in half and peeled; 2 or 3 garlic cloves, peeled; 4 tablespoons (½ stick/55 g) unsalted butter; ½ teaspoon fine sea salt; and a pinch of red pepper flakes (if you like a little spiciness). Cook, stirring and smashing the tomatoes with a wooden spoon every so often, until thick, about 40 minutes. Remove and discard the onion halves. Taste for seasoning, adding more salt if needed. Transfer the cooked ravioli directly to the pot of sauce and toss until coated. You can thin the sauce to your preferred consistency by adding a ladleful of the ravioli cooking water to the pot.

Kimchi

Makes enough to fill one 2-quart (1.9 L) jar

Follow this recipe carefully the first time, then, once you get the hang of it, feel free to experiment by using daikon radish and carrot in place of some of the cabbage, upping the amount of garlic and chile pepper, or adding salted dried shrimp to the mix. Young kimchi is delicious eaten on its own (try it drizzled with toasted sesame oil and sprinkled with sesame seeds), whereas older kimchi works well in fried rice and stir-fries and also tastes great alongside steamed rice (see page 60) and soft-cooked eggs.

1 medium napa cabbage (about 3 pounds/1.4 kg)

½ cup (145 g) fine sea salt

¼ cup (60 ml) fish sauce

¼ cup (25 g) gochugaru (Korean coarsely ground red pepper)

1 (4-inch/10 cm) piece fresh ginger, peeled and finely grated

6 garlic cloves, thinly sliced

1 teaspoon sugar

2 bunches scallions, cut into 1½-inch (4 cm) segments

Cut the cabbage lengthwise into quarters, cut out the core, and slice the quarters crosswise into 2-inch-wide (5 cm) pieces. Place the cabbage in a very large bowl and sprinkle with the salt. Use your hands to mix well, massaging the salt into the cabbage for about 2 minutes. Fill the bowl with enough cold water to submerge the cabbage—it's okay if a few pieces poke out. Set aside to soak for 3 hours.

Drain the cabbage in a colander and rinse thoroughly with cold water. Rinse out the bowl. Squeeze out excess water from the cabbage and return the cabbage to the bowl.

In a medium bowl, mix together the fish sauce, gochugaru, ginger, garlic, and sugar. Add the spices to the bowl with the cabbage, add the scallions, and use your hands to mix well.

Pack the seasoned cabbage into a clean 2-quart (1.9 L) glass jar, pressing down firmly so that the cabbage releases enough of its own liquid and becomes fully submerged. (At first, it won't look like all the cabbage will fit, but it will if you keep packing it in.) Cover with a lid and set aside at room temperature, out of direct sunlight, for 24 hours.

Holding the jar of kimchi over the sink, carefully remove the lid to release the gases that have accumulated. Cover and refrigerate for 1 week before eating. The kimchi will keep well in the refrigerator for months. After about 1 month, it will start to taste more strongly fermented.

A Loaf of Bread

Makes 1 loaf

There's something magical about making bread. You mix together only a few ingredients and give them time and a warm place to rest, and then out of the oven comes this magnificent loaf with a burnished crust and an airy interior. Plan ahead for this recipe, because bread cannot be rushed.

1½ cups (360 ml) lukewarm water

1 teaspoon sugar

1 teaspoon active dry yeast

3 cups (375 g) all-purpose flour, plus more as needed for the dough

1½ cups (170 g) whole wheat flour

2 teaspoons fine sea salt

Olive oil

The night before you want to bake the bread, stir together the water, sugar, and yeast in a large bowl. Cover the bowl with a clean kitchen towel and set aside until tiny bubbles form on the surface of the yeast mixture, about 5 minutes. (If the yeast doesn't foam at all, toss it out and start again with new yeast.) Stir in 2 cups (250 g) of the all-purpose flour. Don't worry about the mixture being smooth—lumps of flour are okay. Cover the bowl with a kitchen towel and let rest at room temperature overnight.

The next day, stir in the remaining 1 cup (125 g) all-purpose flour, the whole wheat flour, and the salt. Turn the dough out onto a clean work surface and knead until satiny and elastic, about 7 minutes. Depending on how humid it is where you live and the time of year, you may need to knead a little more flour into the dough. It should be tacky but not so sticky that it glues itself to your work surface. (Alternatively, you can knead the dough using a stand mixer fitted with the dough hook.)

Lightly grease a large bowl with oil. Add the dough to the bowl, then flip it over and roll it around in the bowl so it's lightly coated with oil. Cover the bowl with a kitchen towel and place in a warm, draft-free spot to rise for 2 hours. (A turned-off oven works well, as does under the covers of a bed.)

Transfer the dough to your work surface. Gently shape it into a tight ball by pulling the edges away from the center, then tucking them under and pinching them firmly together. The surface of the dough should be taut, but be careful not to tear it. Cover the ball of dough with the kitchen towel and let rise on your work surface for 1 hour 30 minutes. ⟶

About 15 minutes before the dough finishes rising, place a Dutch oven with the lid on inside your oven and preheat the oven to 450°F (230°C).

When the dough is ready, use a very sharp knife to slash the top in a few places. Carefully remove the Dutch oven from the oven and gently place the dough inside the Dutch oven. Cover with the lid and bake for 20 minutes. Uncover the Dutch oven and bake until the bread is evenly golden brown, about 20 minutes more. The bottom will sound hollow when knocked. (To test for this sound, carefully flip the bread out of the Dutch oven onto the countertop and use a kitchen towel to flip it right side up. Give the bottom of the bread a knock with your knuckles—be careful, it's hot!—and listen closely for what sounds like hollowness.) Transfer the bread to a wire rack and let cool completely before slicing and serving. During the first few moments of cooling, you can hear the faint, lovely noises of the crust crackling—bakers call this the bread's song.

First Time Kneading Dough? Don't worry if you're unfamiliar with kneading dough—the process is simple and enjoyable: Grab the far edge of the dough, fold the dough over itself toward you, then use the heel of your palm to firmly press the folded dough away from you, stretching it into an oblong shape. Fold it over itself again, rotate it a quarter turn, and press it away from you again. Repeat for many minutes, until the dough has a satisfyingly elastic texture and a satiny surface. You can use a stand mixer fitted with the dough hook to knead the dough, but if you do, be sure to transfer the dough to a work surface for the final minute or two of kneading so you have the pleasure of feeling its smooth, bouncy surface in your own hands.

Shrimp-and-Pork Dumplings

Serves 6 to 8

Gather your friends and family for a dumpling-making party. By the end of all the fun, you'll have enough dumplings to fill your freezer and you'll be stocked up and prepared to make easy, last-minute dinners for a while.

Dumplings

½ pound (225 g) ground pork

½ pound (225 g) raw shrimp, peeled and deveined, then finely chopped

1 small bunch chives, chopped

2 teaspoons finely grated fresh ginger

3 to 4 garlic cloves, minced

2 tablespoons soy sauce

2 teaspoons toasted sesame oil

50 (3½-inch/9 cm) round dumpling wrappers

Dipping Sauce

2 tablespoons soy sauce

1 tablespoon rice vinegar

1 teaspoon toasted sesame oil

1 teaspoon sriracha or sambal oelek (optional)

Make the dumplings: In a large bowl, combine the pork and shrimp. Add all but 1 tablespoon of the chives, the ginger, garlic, soy sauce, and sesame oil. Mix well.

Fill a small bowl with water and set it nearby. Place a dumpling wrapper in the palm of your nondominant hand. Spoon a rounded teaspoon of filling into the center of the wrapper. Dip your finger in the water and use it to moisten the edge of the wrapper. Fold the wrapper in half, around the filling, and pinch the edges closed. Make three pleats on the right side of the curved edge of the dumpling, pinching each pleat firmly to seal, then make three pleats on the left side of the curved edge. The pleats should all point toward the center to give the dumpling a crescent shape. Repeat to form the remaining dumplings.

Make the dipping sauce: In a small bowl, stir together the soy sauce, vinegar, sesame oil, sriracha (if using), and the reserved 1 tablespoon chopped chives.

To cook the dumplings, bring a large pot of water to a simmer. Add the dumplings and cook until you can see the pink color of the shrimp through the wrappers, 3 to 5 minutes. Use a slotted spoon to transfer the dumplings to a shallow bowl. Serve the dipping sauce on the side.

All-Day Roasted Pork

Serves 8 to 12

The amount of hands-on cooking time for this roast seems tiny compared with the amount of succulent meat you end up with. It does take nearly all day to slowly cook (and you'll need to start by seasoning the meat the day before), so be sure to plan accordingly.

¼ cup (50 g) granulated sugar

¼ cup (70 g) plus 2 teaspoons fine sea salt

Freshly ground black pepper

1 (7- to 9-pound/3.2 to 4 kg) whole bone-in, skin-on pork shoulder (sometimes called pork butt)

2 tablespoons rice vinegar or apple cider vinegar

⅓ cup packed (70 g) brown sugar

In a small bowl, mix together the granulated sugar, ¼ cup (70 g) of the salt, and as much pepper as you can stand to grind before your arm hurts.

Place the pork on a rimmed quarter sheet pan or in a roasting pan of similar size. Rub the spice mixture over the pork on all sides. Cover the pork with plastic wrap and refrigerate overnight.

About 15 minutes before you're ready to cook the pork, preheat the oven to 300°F (150°C).

Remove the plastic and transfer the pork to a plate. Rinse the roasting pan, then line it with aluminum foil for easy cleanup. Return the pork to the pan, skin-side up. Roast until extremely tender when poked with a fork, 6 to 7 hours.

Remove the pork from the oven and increase the oven temperature to 500°F (260°C). Spoon out all but about ½ cup (120 ml) of the melted fat from the roasting pan. Keep the excess fat in a heatproof bowl on your countertop in case you want to add some of it back later.

In a small bowl, stir together the vinegar, brown sugar, and remaining 2 teaspoons salt. Brush this glaze on the top and sides of the pork. Return the pork to the oven and roast until it is dark brown and caramelized, about 5 minutes. Serve warm.

Preserved Lemons

Makes enough to fill one 16-ounce (475 ml) jar

Preserving lemons takes nothing more than salt and time. If you put in a few minutes of work at the start of a month, you'll be rewarded with gorgeous jars of preserved lemons by the end of it.

3 to 5 medium lemons

Fine sea salt

1 teaspoon black peppercorns (optional)

1 dried hot chile (optional)

2 bay leaves (optional)

Cut 3 of the lemons from one pointed end down toward the other end, without cutting all the way through, leaving the two halves attached by ½ inch (1.5 cm) or so. Rotate each lemon 90 degrees and make the same cut to create four quarters, still attached at one end. (Each cut lemon will look like a four-petaled tulip.)

Sprinkle a few big pinches of salt into the bottom of a 16-ounce (475 ml) glass jar. Rub a generous amount of salt all over the cut surfaces of the lemons, then shove them into the jar, sprinkling a few big pinches of salt in between each lemon. (It's okay if the lemons break apart into quarters.) Press down firmly on the lemons. They may release enough juice to submerge themselves. If not, squeeze the juice from 1 or 2 more lemons into the jar until the juice completely covers the fruit. Add the peppercorns, chile, and bay leaves, if using. (If you're using a jar that's smaller or larger than 16 ounces/475 ml, you'll need either a few less or a few more lemons to fill it. The important part is only that the lemons are tightly packed in the jar and submerged completely in their juice.)

Cover the jar with a lid and let stand at room temperature for 1 month, shaking and inverting the jar once a day. When finished preserving, the lemon peels will be easily pierced with a fork. Transfer the jar to the refrigerator, where the lemons will keep for up to 1 year.

To cook with preserved lemon, rinse the fruit well and discard the pulp if you don't like its mushy texture. Finely chop or thinly slice the peel and add it to a dish just before serving.

Cooking with Preserved Lemon Any time you want to add a salty, tart kick to a dish, reach for these preserved lemons. Don't toss out the brine left behind in the jar—it makes a tasty addition to savory cocktails like Bloody Marys (page 194).

Apricot Jam

Makes enough to fill six 8-ounce (240 ml) jars

Making jam is really a two-part project. First there's cooking the jam, and then there's preserving it in jars that can be safely stored in your pantry. You can skip the preserving step, if you want, and instead store the jam in your refrigerator, where it will keep well for at least one week. However, preserving can be loads of fun and is easily accomplished with two sets of hands.

3 pounds (1.4 kg) ripe, soft apricots (see note)

4 cups (800 g) sugar

Juice of 1 lemon

Cut each apricot in half and discard the pit. Chop the fruit into 1-inch (2.5 cm) pieces and place in a wide, heavy-bottomed pot. Stir in the sugar and lemon juice. Cover and let stand for at least 30 minutes and up to overnight.

Put two or three small plates in the freezer.

Wash six 8-ounce (240 ml) glass jars and their lids with hot, soapy water. Choose a pot large enough to fit all the jars and tall enough that there can be at least 1½ inches (4 cm) of water above the top of each jar. Fill the pot with water and bring to a simmer. Most jam jars have lids that come apart into two pieces: a flat top and a metal ring. Place the flat tops in a bowl. Carefully lower the glass jars and metal rings into the simmering water to sterilize while you make the jam.

Bring the apricot mixture to a boil over high heat. Cook, stirring frequently and scraping the bottom and sides of the pot with a wooden spoon or heatproof rubber spatula, until the fruit breaks apart and the juices thicken, about 15 minutes. At first the fruit will release a lot of liquid and the jam will look like apricot soup, but don't worry—much of the water will evaporate while the jam cooks. Turn off the heat, then check the jam's consistency by spooning a teaspoon or so onto one of the chilled plates. Return the plate (with the jam on it) to the freezer for 1 minute. Drag your fingertip through the jam—if it stays apart and doesn't run back together, it's done. If the juices spread across the area where you dragged your finger, cook the jam for another few minutes before checking the consistency again. You can also check for doneness by using an instant-read thermometer; as soon as the jam reaches 206°F (97°C), remove the pot from the heat. ⟶

Lift the empty jars out of the simmering water (keep the water at a simmer), allowing them to drain, and place upright next to the stove on a clean kitchen towel. Transfer the metal rings to the bowl with the flat tops, ladle hot water into the bowl, and let sterilize while you fill the jars.

Carefully ladle hot jam into each jar, leaving ¼ inch (6 mm) of headspace at the top of the jar. Using a damp towel, wipe the rims clean. Put the flat tops on the jars, then screw on the metal rings, tightening them only to the point of resistance. Lower the filled jars into the pot of hot water. Simmer for 10 minutes.

Remove the jars from the water and place them on a clean kitchen towel in a spot where they won't be bumped for 12 hours.

After 12 hours, check to make sure each jar sealed properly—the center of the lid should be concave, like a dimple. Any jars that didn't seal should be stored in the refrigerator and eaten within 1 week. Label the sealed jars and store them in your pantry for up to 1 year.

First Time Making Jam? Don't worry at all—apricot is a fantastic fruit to begin with because it contains a high level of natural pectin, meaning you won't need to add anything more than sugar and a splash of lemon juice.

Ripe Apricots Make sure to buy sweet, ripe fruit. If the apricots are still very firm, store them at room temperature and wait until they soften a little before transforming them into jam.

Apple Cider Doughnuts

Makes about ten 3-inch (7.5 cm) doughnuts plus doughnut holes

For the longest time, I couldn't figure out the difference between apple cider and apple juice. Everyone I asked had a different answer. An apple farmer told me they are basically the same, while a chef insisted that cider was by definition unpasteurized. In the grocery store, the two look identical. It turns out there's some variation depending on where you live, but in general, unfiltered apple juice—the cloudy kind often sold in those charming glass jugs with a thumbhole at the top—is indeed the same beverage as apple cider. Boiled until thick and concentrated, it lends its sweetness to these cake doughnuts. Making these doughnuts at home does take some effort, but I've yet to discover a better breakfast than warm apple cider doughnuts and a mug of coffee.

2 cups (480 ml) apple cider or unfiltered apple juice

1 teaspoon cardamom pods

1 teaspoon allspice berries

2 tablespoons ground cinnamon

¾ teaspoon freshly grated nutmeg

3½ cups (440 g) all-purpose flour, plus more for dusting

2 teaspoons baking powder

1 teaspoon baking soda

1 teaspoon fine sea salt

6 tablespoons (¾ stick/85 g) unsalted butter, at cool room temperature

⅓ cup packed (70 g) brown sugar

2 large eggs

½ cup (120 ml) buttermilk

About 2 quarts (1.9 L) neutral-flavored oil, such as canola, for frying

¾ cup (150 g) granulated sugar

Boil the cider in a small saucepan until reduced to ¾ cup (180 ml), 12 to 15 minutes. Let cool while you make the spice mixture.

In a small, dry skillet, toast the cardamom and allspice over medium heat, stirring often, until very fragrant, 3 to 5 minutes. Transfer to a mortar. Peel away and discard the papery pods of the cardamom (you may need to whack each pod with the pestle to crack them open) and flick all the tiny dark seeds into the mortar. Grind the spices to a powder, then stir in the cinnamon and nutmeg.

In a medium bowl, stir together the flour, baking powder, baking soda, salt, and half the spice mixture. (Reserve the remaining spice mixture for the doughnut topping.)

In the bowl of a stand mixer fitted with the paddle attachment, beat the butter and brown sugar together on medium-high speed until light and fluffy, 2 to 3 minutes. Scrape down the sides of the bowl $\longrightarrow$

with a rubber spatula. Add the eggs one at a time, beating well after each addition. Add the buttermilk, boiled cider, and flour mixture. Beat on low speed just until there are no visible streaks of flour remaining. The dough will be soft and sticky. Cover and refrigerate until firm, about 1 hour.

Pour at least 3 inches (7.5 cm) of oil into a heavy-bottomed pot and heat the oil to 350°F (175°C). (If you have a candy thermometer, clip it to the side of the pot so that you can monitor the temperature of the oil and adjust the heat under the pot as needed.)

While the oil heats up, transfer the dough to a generously floured surface. Gently pat it out to ¾ inch (2 cm) thick. Using a 3-inch-diameter (7.5 cm) round cutter and a 1-inch-diameter (2.5 cm) round cutter (or the rims of a water glass and a shot glass), cut out 3-inch-wide (7.5 cm) doughnuts with doughnut holes. You can push the dough scraps together, reroll them, and cut again. The resulting second-round doughnuts might not be quite as tender, but I promise no one will mind. Keep the doughnuts on the floured surface or place them on waxed paper to make sure they don't stick, and don't be shy about dusting them with additional flour.

In a shallow bowl, stir together the remaining spice mixture and the granulated sugar.

When the oil is ready, carefully add 3 or 4 doughnuts to the pot. Fry, flipping once, until they are craggy and a warm dark golden brown color, like redwood bark, about 2 minutes per side. Transfer the fried doughnuts to a wire rack and let cool for 1 minute. While they are still warm, toss the doughnuts in the spiced sugar mixture until evenly coated on all sides. Serve right away (to very lucky guests!) or return them to the rack to cool. Repeat with the remaining doughnuts. Fry all the doughnut holes together as a final batch. The holes will cook a little more quickly, in about 2 minutes, and they don't need to be flipped over. Instead, spin them around in the hot oil and transfer to the rack when they are the same color as the fried doughnuts.

Spiced Orange Bitters

Makes enough to fill one 8-ounce (240 ml) jar

To make bitters, you'll need 100-proof or higher liquor, which, depending on where you live, can be tricky to find. Large liquor stores reliably carry at least a few options. Choose a grain-based alcohol like vodka for clean, neutral flavor. High-proof whiskey and rum will also work to extract aromatic oils—they'll impart their own flavors, but that's not such a problem if you enjoy those flavors. Once you understand the process of making bitters, feel free to experiment using your favorite spices and herbs. Any kind of citrus peel would work in place of the orange in this recipe. Roots of plants like licorice, dandelion, and gentian add powerful and complex bitter aromas. You might also consider making bitters with coffee beans, dried fruits, and flowers.

1 tablespoon allspice berries

1½ teaspoons fennel seeds

1 cinnamon stick

1 orange

4 ounces (½ cup/120 ml) 100-proof or higher liquor (see headnote)

½ cup (120 ml) water

Using a mortar and pestle or the back of a large knife, smash the allspice and fennel a few times to release their aromatic oils. Transfer the spices to an 8-ounce (240 ml) glass jar. Break the cinnamon stick in half and add it to the jar. Remove wide strips of the orange peel using a vegetable peeler, twist the strips into curlicues, and drop them into the jar. Pour in the alcohol. Cover tightly with a lid, label, and store in a dark place for 3 weeks, shaking and inverting the jar once a day or as frequently as you remember.

Strain the mixture through a fine-mesh sieve into a clean jar. Transfer the solids from the sieve to a small saucepan, add the water, and bring to a simmer. Cook gently over low heat, pressing on the spices and peels occasionally, for 5 minutes. Let cool, then strain through the sieve into the jar with the alcohol. You could stop here if you're satisfied with the way the bitters look when you hold the jar up to the light. But since you've come this far, you might as well strain the bitters once more through a coffee filter so that they're super clear. The bitters will keep, tightly covered, at room temperature for years.

Another Way to Enjoy Bitters You know to add bitters to cocktails, but don't forget about their medicinal properties. For a digestive aid after a big meal, stir a few drops of bitters into a glass of sparkling water. You'll feel restored in no time.

Gingerbread People

Makes about fifteen 6-inch (15 cm) cookies

Around the holidays, pick a weekend day to bake a batch of cookies and decorate them for your family and friends. You can cut the cookies into any shape you like. Gingerbread people are classic, while stars and diamonds look lovely and festive.

Cookies

1½ cups (190 g) all-purpose flour, plus more for rolling

1 cup (115 g) whole wheat flour

1 teaspoon fine sea salt

1 teaspoon baking powder

½ teaspoon baking soda

1½ teaspoons ground cinnamon

1½ teaspoons ground ginger

8 tablespoons (1 stick/115 g) unsalted butter, at cool room temperature

½ cup packed (105 g) brown sugar

1 large egg

½ cup (120 ml) molasses

Icing

2 large egg whites

1 teaspoon pure vanilla extract

2½ cups (310 g) confectioners' sugar

Make the cookies: In a medium bowl, stir together the all-purpose flour, whole wheat flour, salt, baking powder, baking soda, cinnamon, and ginger.

In the bowl of a stand mixer fitted with the paddle attachment, beat the butter and brown sugar together on medium-high speed until light and fluffy, about 3 minutes. Scrape down the sides of the bowl with a rubber spatula. Add the egg and molasses and beat until smooth. Add the flour mixture and mix on low speed just until there are no visible streaks of flour remaining. Transfer the cookie dough to a piece of plastic wrap. It will be very sticky and soft. Wrap tightly in the plastic and refrigerate for at least 2 hours and up to 2 days.

When you're ready to bake the cookies, preheat the oven to 350°F (175°C). Line two baking sheets with parchment paper.

On a generously floured surface, roll out the cookie dough to ¼ inch (6 mm) thick. Sprinkle the dough and rolling pin with flour as needed to prevent sticking. Cut into your favorite shapes using a cookie cutter or a knife (see note). Place the cookies on the prepared baking sheets, spacing them at least 1 inch (2.5 cm) apart from one another. (The dough scraps from around the cutout shapes can be rerolled and cut again, but the dough will probably be too soft to easily handle—just chill it in the freezer until firm.) Bake until the cookies feel dry to the touch, 10 to 12 minutes. Let cool for a couple of minutes on the baking sheets, then transfer to a wire rack and let cool completely.

Make the icing: In a large bowl using a handheld mixer or in the bowl of a stand mixer fitted with the whisk attachment, beat the egg whites and vanilla until frothy. With the mixer on low speed, gradually add the confectioners' sugar, then increase the speed to high and beat until stiff and glossy, about 5 minutes. Transfer the icing to a piping bag, or make one yourself by spooning the icing into a plastic bag, twisting the top, and snipping off a corner of the bag (see note).

Decorate the cookies with the icing in any style you like and let set. (You may have some icing left over, but it's always better to have a little extra than not enough.) Once the icing sets and is no longer wet, store the gingerbread cookies in an airtight container at room temperature for up to 3 days.

No Cookie Cutter? If you can't find a cookie cutter in the shape you're looking for, you can draw the outline on a piece of paper, cut it out, place it on top of the rolled-out dough, and trace around it with the tip of a small knife. It's definitely not a perfect system, but it works in a pinch.

No Icing Piping Bag? You can also easily make your own piping bag for the icing. To do so, spoon the icing into a small plastic bag, twist the top while tightly squeezing all the icing down to the bottom of the bag, then use scissors to snip off one corner. If you plan on adding fine features like eyes and mouths for gingerbread faces, snip off only a tiny piece. If you'll be using the icing to fill large areas, snip off a bit more.

Maintaining and Caring for Kitchen Tools

To keep your kitchen tools in fine working order, clean them with care on a regular basis and give them a little extra love every once in a while. Wooden spoons and cutting boards need different maintenance than cast-iron skillets and copper pots do. Here's a rundown of how to care for various tools.

CAST-IRON SKILLETS

Much has been written about how to properly clean a cast-iron skillet. Some cooks are fervent believers in never, ever using soap, while others swear by suds. I fall somewhere in between the two camps. If you roast a chicken in a cast-iron skillet, then I think a mild, soapy wash using a nonabrasive sponge is in order. Whereas if you toast croutons in the skillet, wiping it out with a paper towel seems reasonable to me. Thorough drying, however, is important and universally agreed upon. Do not drip-dry; cast-iron skillets need to be dried by hand with a kitchen towel. For best results, use a paper towel to rub ½ teaspoon of oil into the skillet after it has been dried. (I don't always remember to do so and our skillets are fine, so if you're in a hurry and forget, don't worry about it.) If you come across an old, beat-up cast-iron skillet at a garage sale and would like to revive it, here's how: First scrub away any rust using steel wool and hot, soapy water. (For a badly damaged skillet, you may need to fill it with a mixture of equal parts distilled white vinegar and water, let it stand for 1 hour, then scrub it again.) Give it another soapy rinse. Dip a piece of paper towel in neutral-flavored oil such as canola and rub the inside surfaces of the skillet. Wipe out excess oil, then place the empty skillet in a 500°F (260°C) oven for 1 hour. Carefully remove it and let it cool completely.

WOODEN SPOONS AND CUTTING BOARDS

Wooden cutting boards are preferable to plastic ones for two important reasons: They are easier on your knives, and they're sturdier. You can serve sliced salami directly on the wooden board you cut it on—it will look beautiful, inviting, and rustic. The same cannot be said for plastic. For everyday upkeep of wooden boards and spoons, scrub them with soapy water and dry thoroughly. Never submerge or soak wooden boards in water; use a sponge instead. Make sure you give thick boards a chance to dry evenly on both sides; otherwise, they might warp. Prop them up so air can circulate around both sides until they're completely dry, and remember to flip your primary cutting board over every so often. At least twice a year, take the time to seal and protect your wooden kitchen tools. You can buy food-grade mineral oil for this purpose, but you can also make your own conditioning butter (see at right). Mineral oil is a by-product of refining crude oil to make gasoline, and even though it is labeled "food-grade" here in the United States, it isn't approved for use with food products in the European Union.

CONDITIONING BUTTER

To use this conditioning butter, rub a small amount into the wooden tool or board along the visible grain of the wood. Set the tool or board aside to absorb the butter overnight. The following day, use a clean rag to buff away any excess butter.

Makes 1 cup (240 ml)

6 ounces (170 g) coconut oil
2 ounces (55 g) beeswax

Pour a couple of inches (5 cm) of water into a small saucepan and bring to a simmer over medium heat.

In an 8-ounce (240 ml) glass jar, combine the coconut oil and beeswax. You don't have to be super precise with the weight measurements; it's okay to eyeball a 3:1 ratio of coconut oil to beeswax.

Place the jar in the pan of simmering water and heat gently, stirring as needed to combine, until the beeswax has melted completely and the mixture is clear. Remove the jar from the water and set aside to cool and solidify.

Store, covered with a lid, at room temperature. Conditioning butter will keep for years.

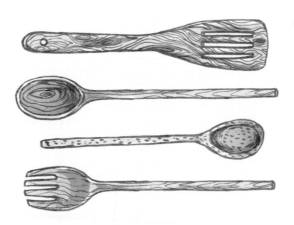

COPPER POTS

Copper will naturally darken with age. Some cooks love this patina and view it as a beautiful mark of quality. Whether you choose to polish your copper is entirely up to you. Restoring its warm glow is as easy as sprinkling salt on a cut lemon half and gently scrubbing the copper. Rinse with soapy water, making sure to use only the soft side of the sponge, and then dry with a soft cloth.

SILVER

Most flatware sold today is made from stainless steel or an amalgam of metals, but you may have been fortunate enough to receive a special family heirloom made of silver or to have found a vintage silver butter dish or cake cutter at an antiques store. Over time, silver tarnishes and develops a dark patina. To polish it to its former glory, first try washing the silver with soapy water and drying it with a soft cloth. That might do the trick. For heavily tarnished silver, try this nontoxic DIY trick: Place the silver pieces you'd like to polish in an aluminum pan (like the kind take-out lasagne comes in) or a pan lined with aluminum foil. Add 1 teaspoon salt and ¼ cup (70 g) baking soda. Pour in enough boiling water to cover. A chemical reaction will occur, transferring the tarnish from the silver to the aluminum. It's important to know that this cleaning technique can remove silver's desirable patina, which is often found within the crevices of decorative carvings, and is also powerful enough to cause pitting in the silver, so some silver aficionados prefer to use store-bought polish. If you're unsure, better to be safe and start with a gentle polish.

STAINLESS STEEL

The key with stainless-steel saucepans and skillets is to never use metal utensils like tongs when cooking in them—they will permanently scratch the surface.

KNIVES

It's important to sharpen your knives when they are dull. There's nothing more frustrating than trying to chop something with a dull blade, and it can also be dangerous because you're more likely to cut yourself when you exert more force on the knife. You could have a professional sharpen your knives, or you can learn to do it yourself at home. For the DIY route, you'll need a whetstone (sometimes called a water stone or sharpening stone). These come in various grit sizes from 100 to 10,000—you should choose a large one (about 8 inches/20 cm long) with a grit size around 1,000. Sometimes the stones will have two sides: a coarser side that's used initially to quickly remove material from your blade, and a finer side that's used next and leads to a sharper blade. Before use, the stone must be submerged in water for about half an hour, until it's fully soaked. Then place it on a kitchen towel that you don't mind using as a rag since it will get quite dirty. The short edge of the stone should face you. Hold the blade of your knife at a 15- to 20-degree angle in relation to the surface of the stone. (No need to overthink it; just hold the blade at

a 45-degree angle and then aim for a little less than half of that.) Starting from the far edge of the stone, drag the blade toward you while simultaneously moving it horizontally along the stone so that the entire blade meets the stone during a single stroke. Repeat this downward stroke motion about thirty times, then flip the knife over and sharpen the other side of the blade, this time starting with the heel of the blade on the side of the stone closest to you and pushing the blade away, toward the top of the stone, moving the knife horizontally just like before. If the stone begins to feel dry, splash it with water. Repeat the strokes on both sides of the knife until the blade is sharp. The entire process could take 15 minutes or more. (It's an excellent time to listen to a podcast!) When you're finished, clean the knife with hot soapy water and rinse off the stone before placing it in a ventilated spot to dry completely. Remember that only straight-edged blades can be sharpened. Serrated knives, unfortunately, cannot, and will dull over time. Keep this in mind when buying knives—put the majority of your budget toward straight-edged knives and know that, with consistent care and upkeep, they will last you a lifetime.

Little Extras

When you are setting up your kitchen and pantry, it's wise and prudent to begin by stocking high-quality everyday essentials like a bottle of extra-virgin olive oil and plenty of fine sea salt. They will demonstrate their value every time you cook with them. As you try out new recipes, you may want to start using a few special ingredients, little extras that aren't strictly necessary. It is becoming easier to find specialty items like candied citrus peel and spice mixes in grocery stores, but they are often expensive. Why not try your own hand at making them? You'll end up with beautiful jars and bottles of delicious foods to add to your dishes. Shelf-stable pantry items like dried fresh herbs, vanilla sugar, and vanilla extract also make lovely gifts. For the little extras that must be stored in the refrigerator, you'll be surprised by how simple they are to make—and how extraordinary they taste when they're homemade.

Refrigerator Pickles

Makes enough to fill one 1-quart (945 ml) jar

If you happen to have a few vegetables that are a little past their prime and need to be used up, pickling them is an easy way to preserve them. Don't bother with canning jars (save your energy for a weekend kitchen project of making jam—see page 249); instead, store these quick pickles in your refrigerator, where they'll keep well for several weeks. You'll have no trouble finding ways to enjoy them, whether you eat them alongside burgers (see page 35) or slice them paper-thin and layer them atop smoked fish on toast or serve them whole with steamed rice and grilled meat. *Pictured on page 268.*

1 cup (240 ml) vinegar (any kind except balsamic; see note)

1 cup (240 ml) water

2 teaspoons sugar

1 teaspoon fine sea salt

4 garlic cloves, halved

6 sprigs thyme

1 bay leaf

1 small dried hot chile, such as chile de árbol

6 black peppercorns

2 cups (300 g) small or sliced vegetables, such as carrots, fennel, green beans, radish, and red onion

In a small saucepan, combine the vinegar, water, sugar, salt, garlic, thyme, bay leaf, chile, and peppercorns. Bring to a boil.

Add the vegetables to the hot brine, one type of vegetable at a time, starting with the hardiest and ending with the least hardy. After each addition, cook until the vegetable is slightly tender but still crisp before adding the next type to the pot. (Carrots and fennel are usually the hardiest and must cook for 1 to 2 minutes, while radish and red onions are often the least hardy and need to cook for only about 30 seconds.) After adding the last type of vegetable, remove the pan from the heat and let the pickles cool to room temperature in the brine.

Transfer the pickles and their brine to a clean 1-quart (945 ml) glass jar. Enjoy them immediately or cover the jar and store in the refrigerator for up to 3 weeks.

Which Vinegar to Use?   Feel free to use any kind of vinegar except balsamic for the pickling brine—red wine, white wine, and apple cider vinegars all work well, and can even be mixed.

Hot Sauce

Makes 1¼ cups (300 ml)

Hot sauce is surprisingly easy to make at home. You might consider making a few different kinds and sharing little bottles of the tastiest batches with friends. (Hot sauce makes a fun Valentine's Day gift!) This recipe relies on dried chiles because they tend to be readily available year-round, and I like their subtle smokiness. *Pictured on page 269.*

5 large or 15 small dried hot chiles

2 garlic cloves

1 teaspoon fine sea salt

¼ cup (60 ml) apple cider vinegar

1 cup (240 ml) boiling water

Tear each chile in half, shake out and discard the seeds (which tend to be bitter), discard the stem, and drop the torn chiles into a dry skillet. Toast over medium-high heat, turning the chiles often, until fragrant and softened, about 2 minutes.

Transfer the toasted chiles to a blender. Add the garlic, salt, vinegar, and water. Blend on high speed until very smooth, about 3 minutes, less if using a powerful blender.

Pour the hot sauce into a glass bottle or jar, cover with a lid, and refrigerate for at least 1 week before using to allow the flavors to marry. The hot sauce will keep well in the refrigerator for months.

Where to Find Dried Chiles? Look for bags of dried chiles at Mexican markets or in specialty food stores (see Resources, page 294), and don't be afraid to experiment with varieties you may not have seen before. Sometimes peppers go by different names when dried. Ancho chile (called poblano when fresh) has a medium heat level. Skinny chile de árbol has a prolonged and intense fieriness. New Mexico chiles are equal parts spicy, sweet, and smoky. Store dried chiles in an airtight container at room temperature and use them within six months, when they're still pliant and shiny.

Whole-Grain Mustard

Makes about 1 cup (240 ml)

Mustards come in a range of flavors and textures. There are spicy canary-yellow ones, thin and pourable. There are chunky whole-grain versions, with tiny brown seeds that pop in your mouth. There are mustards from specific regions in France and Germany and the Netherlands. They all are made from the seeds of the mustard plant, which, depending on the variety, can be yellow (sometimes called white), brown, or black. Once ground, the seeds don't actually taste all that hot. It is only after mixing in a liquid that a chemical reaction occurs, releasing the seeds' volatile compounds. If you add water, the mustard will taste fiery at first, then mellow with time. If you add an acidic liquid like vinegar, you'll end up with a long, slow burn of pungency. This means you can make your own mustard at home to suit your individual preferences. Choose all brown seeds for more zippiness. Or swap the beer in this recipe for water if you like a more mellow mustard. Keep in mind that mustard does take days to make, though most of that time is hands-off. *Pictured on page 268.*

¼ cup (35 g) yellow mustard seeds

¼ cup (35 g) brown mustard seeds

2 tablespoons apple cider vinegar

¾ cup (180 ml) beer

¾ teaspoon fine sea salt

1 tablespoon honey

In a small, nonreactive bowl, combine the yellow mustard seeds, brown mustard seeds, vinegar, and beer. Cover and refrigerate for 2 to 3 days.

Strain through a fine-mesh sieve into a bowl. Transfer the mustard seeds to a food processor or blender. Add the salt, honey, and a splash of the liquid from the bowl. Blend until creamy. If the mustard is thicker than you'd like, add another splash of liquid. Transfer to a glass jar, cover, and refrigerate overnight before using. (It will taste far too bitter immediately after grinding and needs an overnight rest to mellow out.)

The mustard will keep in the refrigerator for at least 1 year.

Lime Crema

Makes about 1 cup (240 ml)

Most recipes for crema, the Mexican version of French crème fraîche, call for mixing buttermilk into cream and then leaving the mixture to thicken at room temperature. It's a cinch to prepare at home and much cheaper than buying premade crema at the store. Make sure you use cream and buttermilk that are *not* ultra-pasteurized—if you use ultra-pasteurized dairy, the crema won't thicken properly. Try drizzling this lime crema over tacos of any kind, including Fried Fish Tacos (page 51) and Carnitas Tacos (page 138). It adds a nice creamy element to pureed soups, and it is also fantastic spread on sandwich bread. *Pictured on page 269.*

1 cup (240 ml) heavy cream (not ultra-pasteurized)

1 tablespoon cultured buttermilk (not ultra-pasteurized)

Zest of 1 lime

¼ teaspoon fine sea salt

In a 16-ounce (475 ml) glass jar, combine the cream and buttermilk. Stir well. Cover with a clean, folded kitchen towel or a piece of cheesecloth and set aside at room temperature, out of direct sunlight, for 24 hours, until thickened.

In a small bowl, use your fingers to combine the lime zest and salt, rubbing to release the zest's fragrant oils. Stir with a spoon into the thickened cream. Cover the crema and store in the refrigerator until ready to use, up to 2 weeks.

What to Do with Extra Buttermilk? After making the crema, you'll be left with lots of buttermilk, since 1 quart (945 ml) seems to be the preferred size for selling buttermilk and this recipe requires only one tablespoon of the sixty-four that make up one quart. Don't worry—the solution is simple: Just make Yeasted Waffles (page 201), and substitute buttermilk for the regular milk.

Aioli

Makes about ¾ cup (180 ml)

If there were ever a recipe meant to be made by a couple, aioli would be it. For one thing, there's a great deal of whisking, and your arm muscles will inevitably tire, so it's wonderful to be able to pass the whisk to your partner and have him or her take over. Also, the bowl tends to move around on the countertop. While one of you whisks, the other can hold the bowl steady. Trade off as often as needed. A kitchen towel, folded and placed underneath the bowl, can also help with wobbliness.

2 or 3 small garlic cloves

Fine sea salt

1 egg yolk

¾ cup (180 ml) olive oil

½ lemon

Using a mortar and pestle or the back of a large knife, pound the garlic and 2 or 3 pinches of salt to a smooth paste.

Place the egg yolk in a medium bowl and whisk to break it up. While whisking continuously, add a few drops of the oil. Whisk until fully incorporated, then add another few drops of the oil. Continue whisking and adding the oil by the drop until the mixture thickens, looks sticky, and pulls away from the sides of the bowl. While whisking continuously, add more oil, this time in a very thin and slow stream. Once you've added somewhere between one-third and half the total oil, squeeze in a little lemon juice to thin the aioli. Add the remaining oil, still in a very thin and slow stream while whisking continuously. The aioli should be as thick as mayonnaise. (If it's not, see the note about how to fix it.)

Stir the garlic paste into the aioli. Taste and adjust the seasoning, adding more salt and lemon juice, if needed. Serve immediately, or cover and refrigerate for up to 1 day.

How to Fix Broken Aioli If the aioli becomes thin and watery, it broke—whoops! Don't worry—you can fix broken aioli like this: Start with a fresh egg yolk in a clean bowl. Follow the recipe as outlined above, but instead of adding oil to the egg yolk, add the broken aioli mixture (first drop by drop, then in a very thin and slow stream) while whisking continuously.

Harissa

Makes ⅔ cup (160 ml)

This spicy, smoky North African chile pepper sauce is made from both dried and fresh peppers. If you're cooking with someone else, one person ought to take charge of the dried chiles and ground spices while the other person prepares the fresh pepper. The two parts come together to make a delicious condiment that's wonderful stirred into a pot of cooked beans, spread on a sandwich, or dabbed on fried eggs. *Pictured on page 269.*

3 dried New Mexico chiles (about 1 ounce/30 g total)

Boiling water

1 large red bell pepper

½ teaspoon caraway seeds

½ teaspoon cumin seeds

3 garlic cloves, peeled

2 tablespoons olive oil, plus more for drizzling

1 teaspoon sherry vinegar

½ teaspoon fine sea salt, plus more as needed

Place the dried chiles in a glass jar or heatproof bowl and pour in enough boiling water to cover. (They'll float, so turn them over occasionally.) Let soak until rehydrated, about 20 minutes.

Meanwhile, roast the bell pepper directly over a gas flame on the stovetop or under the broiler until completely charred, turning the pepper often to evenly char all sides. Transfer the pepper to a paper bag (or place in a bowl and tightly cover with plastic wrap) and let steam for a few minutes. When the pepper is cool enough to handle, peel off and discard the charred skin. Discard the stem and seeds. Resist the temptation to rinse the pepper—it's much better to have a few seeds stubbornly clinging to the pepper than to wash away all those flavorful juices.

In a small skillet, toast the caraway and cumin seeds over medium-high heat. When the seeds begin to pop, remove them from the heat. Grind them using a mortar and pestle or spice grinder.

Drain the soaked chiles. Remove and discard the stems and seeds.

In a blender or food processor, combine the rehydrated chiles, roasted bell pepper, ground spices, garlic, oil, vinegar, and salt. Blend to a thick but smooth sauce. Taste for seasoning, adding salt, if needed.

Transfer the harissa to a clean glass jar, top with a drizzle of oil, cover, and store in the refrigerator for up to 1 month.

Middle Eastern Spice Mix

Makes about 2 tablespoons

You'll get way more flavor from spices if you toast and grind them yourself rather than purchase them preground. That's because, much like dried herbs, spices lose their punch with time. Use this spice mix on popcorn (see page 226), in olive oil (great for dipping warm pita bread in), and as a dry rub for grilled meat and vegetables. *Pictured on page 268.*

1 teaspoon cardamom pods

1 teaspoon black peppercorns

1 teaspoon allspice berries

½ teaspoon whole cloves

1 teaspoon coriander seeds

1 teaspoon cumin seeds

2 teaspoons paprika

Crush the cardamom pods enough to remove their papery green shells. Use your fingertips to scrape all the tiny dark seeds into a small, dry skillet. Add the peppercorns, allspice, cloves, coriander, and cumin. Toast over medium-low heat, shaking the pan every so often, until the spices are fragrant and a shade darker, 4 to 6 minutes.

Using a mortar and pestle or a mini coffee grinder, grind the toasted spices to a coarse powder. Mix in the paprika.

Transfer the spice mix to an airtight container, store at room temperature, and use as soon as possible.

Toasting and Grinding Whole Spices It's easy to toast whole spices—just heat them in a small, dry skillet until they're fragrant and a shade darker. You can use a mortar and pestle to pound them to a coarse powder or grind them in a (clean) mini coffee grinder. They'll leave a faint note of their presence on the grinder and your next batch of ground coffee beans will be perfumed, but it's not such a big deal and can actually be rather nice, depending on the spice. (If the lingering scent does bug you, simply add a handful of uncooked rice to the grinder and blitz until the rice has absorbed the smell.)

A GUIDE TO DRYING FRESH HERBS

Of all the various methods for preserving foods at home, drying herbs might be the easiest and most rewarding.

Start with vibrant, fresh herbs. Those with hardy leaves (oregano, bay, marjoram, rosemary, sage, tarragon, thyme, summer savory) will dry better than those with tender leaves (parsley, cilantro, basil, mint). If you have a garden, the ideal time of day to cut herbs is midmorning, after the dew has evaporated but before the sun is shining directly on the plant. As for the best time of year, you want to aim for the moment when the herb's aromatic oils are most abundant. In the case of lavender, rosemary, sage, and mint, that moment occurs just after the flowers have opened. For most other herbs, however, it's best to cut them before blossoms appear. Leaves aren't the only flavorful part of the plant; flowers and seeds can be dried as well. Caraway, celery, dill, fennel, mustard, cumin, and coriander are great candidates for seed drying.

Gather the herbs into small bunches of four to six sprigs, then strip the leaves from the bottom few inches (7 to 9 cm). If you must wash the herbs, dry them thoroughly to prevent mold growth. Tie each bunch snugly at the base using kitchen twine, string, or a rubber band. (As the herbs dry, they will shrink, so you may have to go back and tighten the knot.) Find a spot outside or inside that is out of direct sunlight and has decent air circulation—attics tend to be terrific—and hang your herb bundles upside down to dry. Depending on the temperature and the herb, this could take anywhere from six days to two weeks. The herbs are fully dried when the leaves crumble easily.

To store your dried herbs, gently pick the leaves (or flowers or seeds) off the stems and place them in a clean glass jar. Label the jar and store it in a dark, cool place. The general rule for cooking with dried herbs goes like this: For every tablespoon of fresh herbs, use only one teaspoon of dried herbs. In other words, dried herbs are three times more powerful than fresh herbs.

Try adding dried thyme to tomato soup (see page 25) or dried oregano to tomato sauce for pizza or pasta. Dried sage complements roasted vegetables of all kinds, particularly winter squashes. You can make wonderfully herby chicken salad using leftover meat from roasted chicken (see page 45) and a big pinch of dried tarragon or summer savory, plus some aioli (see page 273) to bind everything together.

Sugared Rose Petals

Makes about 60 candied petals

The method for making these beautiful, edible candied petals comes from the chefs at Chez Panisse in Berkeley, California. You can use the petals to decorate desserts like Birthday Cake (page 159), or try crumbling them into confetti and scattering them over Classic Vanilla Ice Cream (page 173) like you would rainbow sprinkles. Ask a knowledgeable florist where to find organically grown roses nearby, and choose a variety of colors if you can.

12 organic roses, preferably in a variety of colors

1 or 2 egg whites

Pinch of fine sea salt

Sugar

Gently pluck the individual petals from the roses and pat them thoroughly dry. (The innermost petals are often too curled and tiny for candying—save them to perfume your next bath!)

In a small bowl, whisk 1 egg white and the salt until foamy. Working with 1 rose petal at a time, use a soft-bristled brush to paint both sides of the petal with egg white. Sprinkle a thin layer of sugar evenly over both sides of the petal or dip it in a shallow bowl of sugar. Place the petal on a wire rack and repeat with the remaining petals, spacing them out on the rack so they don't overlap. (If you run out of egg white, just add a second egg white to the bowl and whisk in another pinch of salt. Depending on the size of your roses, you may need only 1 egg white.) Let the candied petals dry at room temperature overnight, or until crisp.

Store in an airtight container in the refrigerator for up to 1 week.

VANILLA SUGAR AND VANILLA EXTRACT

Using whole vanilla beans is a wonderful way to add a wallop of pure vanilla flavor to all sorts of dishes like pudding, ice cream (see page 173), dainty madeleine cookies, cake, and much more. The beans can be expensive, though, so I'm always searching for ways to make them go further by eking out as much flavor as possible.

One way you can do this is to use the beans that you've already split and scraped clean of their sticky vanilla seeds. Those spent pods still contain loads of flavor. Stick them into a glass jar of granulated sugar, shake to distribute, and then cover tightly and store in your pantry. The sugar will take on a marvelous vanilla aroma. It's delicious stirred into coffee, sprinkled over strawberries, and used in place of regular sugar in pretty much any dish. When the sugar level in the jar dips low, refill it with more sugar. Continue adding spent vanilla beans to the jar whenever you have them.

Another way to use the precious beans is to make your own vanilla extract. Find an empty little glass bottle and clean it thoroughly. As a rule of thumb, you'll need ¾ cup (6 ounces/180 ml) alcohol for every 4 vanilla beans. You can use any strong alcohol, but choose a mildly flavored one such as white rum or vodka so it won't obscure the flavor of the vanilla. Use the tip of a small knife to split each bean lengthwise, then drop them into the bottle and pour in enough alcohol to cover. Seal tightly and store out of direct sunlight for about 2 months. During that time, whenever you think of it, shake the bottle gently.

You can start using the extract after only 3 or 4 weeks if you'd like a delicate vanilla aroma. The longer the extract sits, the more robustly flavored it will become. It essentially never spoils; I once discovered a many-years-old bottle of vanilla extract that I had made and stashed at the back of my parents' kitchen cupboard, and it was more aromatic than any I've ever smelled. Bottles of vanilla extract make such thoughtful gifts for those who love to bake. Around Halloween, when you're carving pumpkins, try to remember to make a few bottles of vanilla extract so they'll be ready to give to family and friends for the holidays.

Candied Grapefruit Peel and Grapefruit Syrup

Makes about 4 cups (400 g) peel and about 1 cup (240 ml) syrup

It might seem like grapefruit syrup is merely a by-product of making candied grapefruit peel, but in fact the syrup alone is worth your effort. Grapefruit syrup will keep for at least a month, and you can use it in many ways. Stir it into sparkling water for refreshing homemade soda. Add it to a cocktail like the Paloma (page 115). Make a cordial by mixing syrup and fresh grapefruit juice. It's also wonderful spooned over ripe berries and plain yogurt. *Pictured on page 280.*

2 large grapefruits (see note)
2 cups (400 g) sugar, plus more for coating
1 cup (240 ml) water

Cut the grapefruits in half through their middles and juice them. Enjoy the juice in a glass with a few ice cubes (or save it for a cocktail).

Place the grapefruit halves in a medium saucepan, cover with cold water, and bring to a boil. Drain. Cover with fresh cold water, bring to a boil, and drain again. Repeat once more, this time boiling the fruit until the peels are soft when prodded with a fork, about 15 minutes. Drain and let cool.

Using a sturdy spoon, scrape out and discard the pulp. Some grapefruits will hold on to more of their spongy white pith than others. Just make sure there's no more than ¼ inch (6 mm) of white pith remaining, or the candied peels will taste too bitter. Cut the scraped peels into long strips about ¼ inch (6 mm) wide.

Return the peels to the saucepan. Add the sugar and water. Simmer over medium-low heat, stirring every so often, until the peels are translucent, 20 to 25 minutes.

Using tongs or a slotted spoon, lift the peels out of the hot syrup and spread them in a single layer on a wire rack set inside a rimmed baking sheet. Let the peels cool at room temperature for 2 hours. Toss them in sugar until they're coated, then store in an airtight container at room temperature for several months.

Store the grapefruit syrup in a glass jar in the refrigerator for up to 1 month. (You can strain it first if you prefer, but you don't have to.)

For Other Types of Citrus Fruit You can use this method to candy any type of citrus fruit, including oranges, limes, and Meyer lemons. Grapefruits are particularly tasty because they have a lovely bitter note that contrasts well with the sweetness of sugar. (If you don't use grapefruits, skip step two, in which you drain off the boiling water—that part of the recipe helps temper the fruit's bitterness.)

A Sweet Gift This recipe yields exactly the right amount of candied peel to fit inside a 1-quart (945 ml) glass jar (minus a few that you'll need to taste for quality control), and therefore makes a pretty gift.

Variation

CHOCOLATE-DIPPED CANDIED PEEL

Place 8 ounces (225 g) dark chocolate, chopped into small pieces, in a heatproof bowl. Bring about 1 inch (2.5 cm) of water to a simmer in a small sauce pot. Set the bowl of chocolate over the pot, making sure the bottom of the bowl doesn't touch the water. Heat gently, stirring occasionally, until the chocolate is melted and smooth. Remove the bowl from the heat. Dip each candied grapefruit peel about halfway into the chocolate, allowing any excess chocolate to drip back into the bowl. Place the dipped candied peel on a parchment paper–lined baking sheet and let stand at room temperature until firm, about 24 hours.

Common Cooking Issues and How to Fix Them

Don't worry if you goof up and something goes awry. There's almost always a fix, or at least a clever way to disguise the problem. Remember that you shouldn't apologize for food you've cooked; doing so only draws attention to something your spouse or guests probably wouldn't otherwise have noticed. Any time you need to, consult this list of common cooking issues and their fixes.

A Cutting Board That Slides Around

Place a clean kitchen towel underneath the board. Fold over the edges of the towel as needed to keep them from peeking out. You shouldn't be able to see the towel, but you'll feel it working the next time you slice a loaf of bread.

A Cooking Tools Drawer That Resembles a Junk Drawer

Handheld cooking tools can be surprisingly cumbersome for their size. Pile them together in a pull-out kitchen drawer and you'll end up with teaspoons stuck inside a whisk and a jumble of other problems. Storing them in this manner risks damaging the tools. More important, it's not enjoyable to wade through an assortment of semi-sharp can openers in a desperate search for a metal spatula. Start by removing all the cooking tools from the drawer. (Wipe out any crumbs while it's empty.) Toss out every tool that doesn't work. If you have duplicate tools—say, two rubber spatulas or three vegetable peelers—donate the spares. Gather all the wooden tools and place them upright in a container on your kitchen counter like a bouquet of flowers. We use one of those sturdy, thick-rimmed, diner-style coffee mugs to hold them all within arm's reach of the stove. Measure and cut a thin piece of corkboard to line the bottom of the kitchen drawer. This will prevent the tools from sliding around and colliding with one another. Cork also naturally resists the growth of mold and mildew. Put your newly curated selection of tools back in the drawer, finding a spot for each one on the corkboard and avoiding overcrowding them.

Catching Lemon Seeds

When squeezing juice from a lemon, you don't need to use a special tool—just hold your other hand under the lemon, with your fingers pressed together and palm cupped slightly. You'll catch the seeds in your palm and the lemon juice will strain through the gaps between your fingers.

Eggshells Falling into the Bowl

Use the half eggshell in your hand to scoop up any little pieces of shell that might have fallen into the bowl. Next time you crack an egg, do it on a flat surface like a kitchen countertop rather than on the edge of a bowl, and it will crack cleanly into two halves. You could also crack the egg into a small bowl before adding it to whatever you're cooking. That way, it's easier to fish out stray shell pieces.

Broken Aioli

See page 273. There's also a neat trick for keeping the bowl steady while you're whisking the aioli.

Burnt Piecrust

Keep an eye on your pie when it is close to done. If the crust is browning too quickly, cover it with aluminum foil. You can shape a ring out of foil and cover just the edges of the crust if the middle could use a little more browning. When you take the baked pie out of the oven, if the crust is mahogany brown, that is wonderful—all that caramelization will taste great. If it's truly burnt, use a serrated knife to scrape off any black parts, then just obscure the darkened crust by serving each piece of pie topped with a generous amount of whipped cream.

Dry Cake

Whoops, your cake came out of the oven overcooked and too dry. You can easily remedy this situation by making a simple syrup to drizzle over the cake. Combine equal parts granulated sugar and fresh citrus juice (from oranges, lemons, limes, or a combination) in a small pot and bring to a simmer, stirring to dissolve the sugar. Use a toothpick or the tines of a fork to poke many holes in the dry cake, then spoon the syrup over the cake and let it soak in.

Cake Stuck to the Pan

When you invert a baked cake out of its pan and some of the cake sticks to the pan, use a butter knife to unstick the cake pieces from the pan and then put them back where they belong in the cake. You can cover the top with frosting or simply serve it upside down. If the cake is so stuck to the pan that it seems like a true mess, turn it into a variation on a dish called Eton Mess—layers of fresh fruit, broken pieces of cake, and spoonfuls of barely sweetened whipped cream (see page 174) served in a tall glass or a trifle dish.

Undercooked Meat

This one's no issue at all—just put the meat back in the skillet, into the oven, or onto the grill and cook for another minute or two. Remember to let it rest once again before slicing. It might not be quite as juicy as it would have been, but you'll probably be the only one who notices.

Overcooked Meat or Fish

Shred or cut the meat or fish into small pieces and mix them into plenty of rich, flavorful sauce. Pork and beef are great stirred into Harissa (page 274), fish works well in Herb Sauce (see page 131), and chicken can be transformed into creamy chicken salad (see page 46).

Food That Is Too Spicy

One way to counteract tongue-tingling spiciness is to introduce a mellowing dairy ingredient. If a curry is too fiery, try adding a splash of coconut milk. For tomato sauce made with a few too many red pepper flakes, stir in some heavy cream.

Food That Is Too Salty

Try to increase the volume of the dish, thereby diluting the salt. Add water to soups, broths, and stews; whisk olive oil and lemon juice into salad dressings and herb sauces; and if you're cooking a dish like Stovetop Popcorn (page 226), see if you can make more popcorn and add it to the batch that's oversalted.

Not Enough Food for Guests

It can be difficult to estimate how much food to cook for guests, especially if you're having many people over. It just takes some practice to develop this skill. Always plan for a little more than you think people will eat. If a few extra guests join the dinner party, try adding a loaf of bread (keep a spare in the freezer for reheating) or another stack of tortillas or another pot of rice to the meal. Depending on the dish you're cooking, you might add a few more potatoes to the soup or another head of lettuce to the salad. If you have a small enough group and they've eaten everything at the table, you can relatively quickly cook an omelet (page 193) for each person. Customize each omelet and it'll feel special. One more fun option: Do like the Italians and make *spaghettata*, a dish formally called *spaghettata di mezzanotte*, or "midnight spaghetti," because it's enjoyed late at night, after a party, when you're not quite ready to go to bed. To cook it, make a simple sauce for pasta using flavorful pantry essentials you have on hand: anchovies, canned tomatoes, capers, even seasoned bread crumbs. Or follow the recipe on page 30.

Red Beet Marks on a Cutting Board

All you need are hot, soapy water, a sponge, and some elbow grease. Scrub until the marks disappear.

Garlic and Onion Scents Stubbornly Lingering on a Cutting Board

Sprinkle lots of salt across the board. Cut a lemon in half and rub the cut sides over the board. The salt will act as a natural abrasive and the lemon juice will clean away the lingering scents. Wash the board with hot, soapy water and dry thoroughly.

Cooking Smells in the Air

Bring a small saucepan of water to a simmer. Use a vegetable peeler to remove a few wide strips of zest from a citrus fruit. Drop the zest into the pot of water and simmer for several minutes, until the smell in the air neutralizes. If that doesn't do the job, add a few tablespoons of distilled white vinegar to the pan and simmer until the air is clear.

Wedding Registry Checklist

Here are the kitchen tools and entertaining goods mentioned and recommended throughout this book, all in one place for you to reference as you put together your wedding registry. When considering which gifts you'd be thrilled to receive, you and your fiancé(e) should first take stock of what you already own. Customize the following checklist by crossing off anything you have or won't need, and feel free to add additional items to "My Checklist," opposite. The tools and goods are grouped together by category and, within each category, the items are listed in order of importance. If you're curious about what to look for when selecting kitchen equipment and tools, see pages 13 to 17. For more information about setting the table, see pages 54 to 55, and for more about stocking your home bar, see pages 108 to 111.

KITCHEN EQUIPMENT AND TOOLS

- ☐ Wooden cutting board
- ☐ Large knife
- ☐ Cast-iron skillet
- ☐ Kitchen towels
- ☐ 18 by 13-inch (46 by 33 cm) rimmed baking sheet
- ☐ Mixing bowls
- ☐ Measuring spoons and cups
- ☐ 6- to 8-quart (6 to 8 L) heavy-bottomed pot
- ☐ 1- to 2-quart (1 to 2 L) saucepan
- ☐ Wooden spoons
- ☐ Colander
- ☐ Tongs
- ☐ Whisk
- ☐ Rasp-style grater
- ☐ Box grater
- ☐ Pepper grinder
- ☐ Vegetable peeler
- ☐ Small knife
- ☐ Mortar and pestle
- ☐ Serrated bread knife
- ☐ Fine-mesh sieve
- ☐ Wire rack
- ☐ Metal spatula

- ☐ Ladle
- ☐ 9 by 13-inch (23 by 33 cm) rimmed baking sheet
- ☐ Stand mixer or electric beaters
- ☐ Immersion or countertop blender
- ☐ Rolling pin
- ☐ 9-inch (23 cm) round cake pans
- ☐ Muffin tin
- ☐ Pie plate
- ☐ 4½ by 8½-inch (11 by 21 cm/1.5 L) loaf pan
- ☐ Rubber spatula
- ☐ Food processor
- ☐ Dutch oven
- ☐ Instant-read thermometer
- ☐ French steel pan
- ☐ Salad spinner
- ☐ Ice cream scoop
- ☐ Pastry brush
- ☐ Spider strainer/skimmer
- ☐ Food scale
- ☐ 12-inch (30 cm) stainless-steel sauté pan
- ☐ 3-quart (3 L) saucepan
- ☐ Coffee bean grinder

ENTERTAINING GOODS

☐ Plates
☐ Flatware: forks, knives, spoons
☐ Water glasses
☐ Cloth napkins

☐ Platters
☐ Serving spoons
☐ Coffee mugs and/or teacups
  and saucers

HOME BAR

☐ Bottle opener and waiter's
  friend–style corkscrew
☐ Ice cube tray
☐ Rocks glasses
☐ Cocktail shaker
☐ Muddler

☐ Jigger
☐ Highball glasses
☐ Wineglasses
☐ Beer glasses
☐ Coupe glasses

MY CHECKLIST

☐ ....
☐ ....
☐ ....
☐ ....
☐ ....
☐ ....
☐ ....
☐ ....
☐ ....
☐ ....
☐ ....
☐ ....
☐ ....
☐ ....
☐ ....
☐ ....
☐ ....

☐ ....
☐ ....
☐ ....
☐ ....
☐ ....
☐ ....
☐ ....
☐ ....
☐ ....
☐ ....
☐ ....
☐ ....
☐ ....
☐ ....
☐ ....
☐ ....
☐ ....

Our Favorite Recipes

Parties We've Hosted

Funny Stories from Around Our Table

Resources

Ingredients

ANCHOVIES AND SARDINES

The Spanish Table
1814 San Pablo Avenue
Berkeley, CA 94702
spanishtable.com

CHEESE

Cowgirl Creamery Cheese Shop
1 Ferry Building, 17
San Francisco, CA 94111
cowgirlcreamery.com

Laura Chenel's Chèvre, Inc.
22085 Carneros Vineyard Way
Sonoma, CA 95476
laurachenel.com

Murray's
254 Bleecker Street
New York, NY 10014
murrayscheese.com

CHOCOLATE AND COCOA POWDER

Guittard Chocolate Company
10 Guittard Road
Burlingame, CA 94010
guittard.com

Valrhona
222 Water Street
Brooklyn, NY 11201
valrhona-chocolate.com

COCKTAIL CHERRIES (AMARENA CHERRIES)

Market Hall Foods
5655 College Avenue
Oakland, CA 94618
markethallfoods.com

DRIED BEANS AND GRAINS

Anson Mills
ansonmills.com

Rancho Gordo
1924 Yajome Street
Napa, CA 94559
ranchogordo.com

DRIED PASTA

Baia Pasta
431 Water Street
Oakland, CA 94607
baiapasta.com

FLOUR

King Arthur Flour
kingarthurflour.com

JAM AND PRESERVES

Sqirl
720 Virgil Avenue, #4
Los Angeles, CA 90029
sqirlla.com

OLIVE OIL

California Olive Ranch
californiaoliveranch.com

PROSCIUTTO, SALUMI, AND OTHER CURED MEATS

Fra' Mani Handcrafted Foods
1311 Eighth Street
Berkeley, CA 94710
framani.com

La Quercia
laquercia.us

ROSE WATER

King Arthur Flour
kingarthurflour.com

Sahadi's
187 Atlantic Avenue
Brooklyn, NY 11201
sahadis.com

SALT AND SPICES

Diaspora Co.
diasporaco.com

Kalustyan's
123 Lexington Avenue
New York, NY 10016
kalustyans.com

Maldon Salt Company
maldonsalt.co.uk

Penzeys Spices
penzeys.com

Zingerman's
zingermans.com

TEA

August Uncommon Tea
august.la

Mariage Frères
mariagefreres.com

WINE

Kermit Lynch Wine Merchant
1605 San Pablo Avenue
Berkeley, CA 94702
kermitlynch.com

Home and Kitchen Supply Stores

Anthropologie
anthropologie.com

Brook Farm General Store
brookfarmgeneralstore.com

Crate & Barrel
crateandbarrel.com

Food52
food52.com

Healdsburg Shed
25 North Street
Healdsburg, CA 95448
healdsburgshed.com

Heath Ceramics
2900 18th Street
San Francisco, CA 94110
heathceramics.com

Indigo
chapters@indigo.ca

Kaufmann Mercantile
kaufmann-mercantile.com

March
3075 Sacramento Street
San Francisco, CA 94115
marchsf.com

Muji
muji.us

**Schoolhouse Electric
& Supply Co.**
2181 NW Nicolai Street
Portland, OR 97210
schoolhouse.com

Sur La Table
surlatable.com

Williams Sonoma
williams-sonoma.com

Recommended Cookware Brands

All-Clad
all-clad.com

Bialetti
bialetti.com

Breville
breville.com

Cuisinart
cuisinart.com

Duralex
duralexusa.com

Emile Henry
emilehenryusa.com

Hess
hesspottery.com

KitchenAid
kitchenaid.com

Le Creuset
lecreuset.com

Lodge Cast Iron
lodgemfg.com

Mauviel
mauvielusa.com

OXO
oxo.com

Riedel
riedel.com/en-us

Rösle
roesle.com/us

Vitamix
vitamix.com

Wüsthof
wusthof.com

Zwilling J. A. Henckels
zwilling.com/us

Online Gift Registries

Blueprint Registry
blueprintregistry.com

MyRegistry
myregistry.com

Thankful Registry
thankfulregistry.com

Zola
zola.com

Acknowledgments

I am incredibly fortunate to have my name on the cover, but there are many, many people who worked behind the scenes to bring this book to life.

Thank you to my literary agent and dear friend Katherine Cowles for inspiring this project and expertly shepherding it from start to finish. I am honored to be counted among your authors and I still pinch myself to make sure this isn't all just a dream.

The recipes in this cookbook were carefully tested in home kitchens across the country by a group of wonderful people affectionately known as the Testing Team. Thank you to Aaron Shinn and Gina Zupsich, Akemi Martin, Amanda and Jared Heinke, Ashley Quinn, Cameron Toler, Carla Inouye, Cat Dailey Minyard, Christine Binder, Dean Mingus, Dervla Kelly, Devan Gregori, Ed Dailey, Emily Rusca, Erin Ferguson and Kevan Warren, Hannah Davitian, Hanna Reichel, Hannah Robie, Hannah Vaughan, Heather Platt, Hollie Loson, Ileana Morales Valentine, Jena Umfress, Jennifer and Ben Naecker, Jessica and Jeff Naecker, Joanna Evans and Alec Levy, Jocelyn Bradley, Julia Wardega, Juliana Stone, Julianne Mesaric, Julie Beigel-Coryell, Kathy and Michael Brew, Kelli Abrahamian, Kristin Jacobson, Lauren May, Lisa Wahl, Maia Piccagli, Maïalène Wilkins, Mallory Rakay, Mary Zaletel, Molly Rubin, Natasha Nicolai, Nina Stössinger, Pam White, Rachel and David Hochstetler, Risa Vierra, Robin Hinesley Bradley, Sarah Cotey, Sarah Fisher, Sofia Martin, Tânia Raposo, Ted Zika, Tracey Landstrom, Wendy Lee and Nick Snead, and Yahli Eshel.

Mark Dingo Francisco, thank you for all your gorgeous illustrations, and for your steadfast optimism and willingness to work so swiftly. Even though you and I live sixteen times zones apart, your upbeat and reassuring emails somehow made it feel like we were next-door neighbors. Thanks also to Tobias Frere-Jones for Mallory, the typeface that makes the recipes look both elegant and friendly.

I will forever be grateful to our photo crew, led by Aya Brackett, photographer extraordinaire. Aya, I can't begin to describe how excited I was to collaborate with you after having admired your painterly photographs for years. Little did I know that your spirit is as beautiful as your work. I'm already looking forward to working together again in the future. Thank you to photo assistants and digital techs Summer Wilson and Mike Byrne; prop stylist Claire Mack and fabricator/scenic painter David Gantz, who together own Rule&Level Studio in Berkeley, California; food stylist Abby Stolfo; and kitchen assistants Taylor Schwartz and Julia Middleton. Heartfelt thanks to my friend Sarah Weiner for welcoming us with open arms into her lovely cottage for a full day of photography.

Thank you very much to the hardworking team at Artisan Books: editor Judy Pray, who was the indefatigable and keen captain of this ship, steering us always in the right direction; editorial assistant Bella Lemos; creative director Michelle Ishay-Cohen; publisher Lia Ronnen; copy editor Ivy McFadden; production editor Sibylle

Kazeroid; design manager Jane Treuhaft; the production team of Nancy Murray and Hanh Le; and managing editor Zach Greenwald.

I never would have had the opportunity to write this book if it weren't for Suzanne Goin. She took a chance on me when I was a graduate student and has been the greatest supporter of my career ever since. Suzanne, you are—and always will be—my hero. Thank you for your friendship, mentorship, guidance, and love. Thank you for teaching me so much about cooking but also about life. When I get stuck on something, I always think, *What would Suzanne do?* And when I overcome something that is daunting, it is because you have led the way by example, showing not just me but many others as well how to be courageous and generous and graceful at all times, particularly in the face of difficulty.

Thank you to the many talented chefs I've had the pleasure of working with and learning from, especially Elisabeth Prueitt, Chad Robertson, Christina Tosi, Alice Waters, Russell Moore, Jessica Koslow, Deborah Madison, and Yotam Ottolenghi. You have shaped the way I think about food in more ways than you'll ever know.

My sincerest thanks to friends and family whose acts of encouragement buoyed me and propelled me forward in the making of this book: Chloe Sorvino, Kristen Miglore, Zuzana Licko, Rudy VanderLans, Jessica L'Esperance and Isaac Dietz (and to Iris and Albert for being such joyful taste testers), Daisy and Greg Ryan (and Henry, too!), Kate Lydon, James Bradley, Reed Bradley, Nancy and Gerald Frazee, Daniela Bongers, and Tim Bradley. To my mother-in-law, Marla Frazee, you are an inspiration and a model for all young people who want to grow up and become authors. I can hardly believe my good fortune to have you in my life. Thank you for cheering me on, looking out for me, and always having my back. Thank you to my wonderful parents, Ellie Blakely Zizka and George Zizka, for your endless love. You've demonstrated time and time again that two people who love and support each other can accomplish just about anything—in and out of the kitchen. I love you very much.

Most of all, thank you to my husband, Graham Bradley, who is the greatest love of my life and who has always believed in me. When we first met as college kids, we dreamed of one day working together on a cookbook. I knew you'd design it beautifully, with such skill and brilliance, but I wasn't so sure of my own abilities to write it. You supported me, championed my work each step of the way, inspired new recipes, read and edited every single bad draft I wrote, encouraged me when I needed it, and gave me the confidence to keep going—all while doing the hard work of designing everything from the overall page layout to the smallest details like the arrow that indicates a recipe continues on the following page. Without you, this book wouldn't exist. It is as much yours as it is mine, and I am so proud of all that we've created together. Thank you for being you and thank you for loving me.

Index

Maria Zizka, named by *Forbes* as one of the most influential people under 30 in the world of food and drink, is the coauthor of numerous award-winning cookbooks, most recently *Tartine All Day* and *Everything I Want to Eat*. She and her husband live and cook together in Berkeley, California.